PLYMOUTH ARGYLE
Miscellany

PLYMOUTH ARGYLE
Miscellany

*Pilgrims Trivia,
History, Facts & Stats*

RICK COWDERY & MIKE CURNO

PLYMOUTH ARGYLE
Miscellany

All statistics, facts and figures are correct as of 5th May 2009

© Rick Cowdery and Mike Curno

Rick Cowdery and Mike Curno have asserted their rights in accordance with the Copyright, Designs and Patents Act 1988 to be identified as the author of this work.

Published By:
Pitch Publishing (Brighton) Ltd
A2 Yeoman Gate
Yeoman Way
Durrington
BN13 3QZ

Email: info@pitchpublishing.co.uk
Web: www.pitchpublishing.co.uk

First published 2009
Reprinted 2015

All rights reserved. No part of this publication may be reproduced, stored in a retrieval system, or transmitted in any form or by any means, electronic, mechanical, photocopying, recording or otherwise, without the prior permission in writing of the publisher and the copyright owners.

A catalogue record for this book is available from the British Library.

ISBN: 978-1-9054114-0-5

Typesetting and origination by Pitch Publishing
Printed and bound in India by Replika Press Pvt. Ltd.

This book is dedicated to
colleagues and friends at Home Park,
and to the rest of the Green Army.

Rick Cowdery and Mike Curno, August 2009

FOREWORD BY DANNY SALMAN

I'VE always thought that, if you want to know anything about Argyle, you could do a lot worse than ask Rick Cowdery. I've known Rick since the day I arrived at Home Park – he interviewed me in the dressing-room – and I haven't quite been able to shake him off since. Now that I've retired from playing and am working for the Press Association on matchdays, we share the Home Park Press Box.

Seriously, though, what he doesn't know about Argyle probably isn't worth knowing. Since this is a trivia book, let me tell you a small piece of previously unpublished trivia that links me, Rick, Argyle and Peter Shilton.

Shortly after Peter took over as manager at Home Park, he suddenly dropped me from the starting XI, having previously used me as sweeper for his first few games. When I found out on the Thursday that I wouldn't be playing on the Saturday, I was naturally unhappy and Rick, sensing my annoyance, asked me what was up. I told him, and he duly reported in his *Western Morning News* column that Shilts was going to give the sweeper system the brush-off.

As a good journalist, he didn't name his source, i.e. me, and still refused to reveal it when the manager hauled him into his office and over the coals the following week. Even though it made his relationship with Shilton nigh-on impossible from then on, Rick ensured my identity remained secret. Until now.

It was another small storyline from the soap opera called 'Football' that we all love watching, and there are lots more similar vignettes, lovingly compiled by Rick and Mike Curno, in the pages that follow from episodes set at Home Park over the years. I know you will enjoy them. I did.

Danny Salman,
Plymouth Argyle 1990-92

ACKNOWLEDGEMENTS

The authors would like to thank to all those at Pitch Publishing, most notably Dan Tester, for his guidance and patience. A huge debt of gratitude goes, as usual, to all the Argyle experts whose own love for the Pilgrims has provided valuable sources of reference in many works and websites, notably Steve Dean, Harley Lawer, Peggy Prior and Andy Riddle. Thanks, too, to Mr Goals, Dave Rowntree, for his pictures.

Rick Cowdery and Mike Curno, August 2009

INTRODUCTION

Plymouth Argyle Miscellany is a book you can easily live without. Although, if you have even the slightest interest in Plymouth Argyle, you will not want to.

Otherwise, how will you discover which Greens forward loved to let young children swing from his outstretched arms? Or which Pilgrim became a saint by saving a baby from drowning? Or how long Sean McCarthy wore his undergarments before celebrating his 200th goal? All trivial stuff, but, somehow, so important.

There have been more than a few books written about Argyle, and this one complements them all by mixing lightly frothy facts like the above with some seriously weighty stats covering all the major moments in Argyle's history: runs and records, games and gates, cups and ups and downs.

Your coffee table will love it. A couple of pieces of housekeeping: to help identify which tier of the English League system Argyle were in at any given time, you need to familiarise yourself with http://en.wikipedia.org/wiki/The_Football_League.

Also, all the facts and figures are up to date as far as May 5th, 2009. To that end, where, for instance, a player has remained at the club past that date, his stats will still be concluded with a "-2009". Please bear that in mind when enjoying the following.

Rick Cowdery and Mike Curno, August 2009

TWO LEE HODGES...

CONFUSINGLY for future Argyle historians, the Pilgrims had two players called Lee Hodges who played for them between 1993-2008, both Londoners who previously played for London clubs, and both of whom played in midfield for the Greens. Lee Hodges I (b. Epping) was signed on loan from Tottenham Hotspur by Peter Shilton in 1993 and scored twice in seven Barclays Second Division games. He netted what turned out to be the winner in a 2-1 victory at Chester City on February 27th and followed that up with the opener in the following week's 4-0 triumph over Preston North End. Interestingly, both matches included own goals for the Pilgrims. Lee Hodges II (b. Newham) was also a loan acquisition, from West Ham United, for Mick Jones midway through the 1997/1998 Nationwide Second Division season which ended in relegation. He played in ten games, without scoring, making his debut in a 3-0 victory over AFC Bournemouth on November 8th, 1997. In 2001, Lee Hodges I returned to Home Park at the start of the 2001/02 Nationwide Third Division season and became an integral part of the Pilgrims' post-millennium rise through the divisions. Although the Lee Hodgeses never played together, they did feature on the same pitch, when the Pilgrims lost 2-1 at Scunthorpe United's Glanford Park just before Christmas 2001. The match brought to an end Argyle's 19-game undefeated run, a club record for a single season that had stretched back to late August. Inevitably, given the immutable Law of the Former Player, Lee Hodges II scored both Scunthorpe goals.

MR BROWN, YOU'VE GOT A LOVELY SON

AS well as having two Lee Hodgeses, Argyle have also had two Ken Browns. Ken Brown senior was the Pilgrims' manager for two Barclays League Second Division seasons between the summer of 1988 and February 1990, during which time he signed his son, also called Ken (or, often, to avoid too much confusion, 'Kenny') from Norwich City, the club that had sacked Ken senior prior to his appointment at Home Park. Ken junior outlasted his father by 15 months, was a virtual ever-present for three seasons, and was voted Player of the Season by the Green Army for the 1990/91 Barclays Second Division campaign before moving on to West Ham United... the club for which Ken senior had played between 1952-67.

LEE HODGES: OR LEE HODGES J, TO GIVE HIM HIS FULL NAME

YOU NEED HANDS

WHEN Argyle goalkeeper Luke McCormick was sent off in the 71st minute of the Pilgrims' 2007-08 Championship game at Scunthorpe United's Glanford Park, it was the moment that Lee Hodges had been dreading for six seasons. Midfielder Hodges had been Argyle's designated replacement custodian in the absence of any keeper on the substitutes' bench since his arrival at Home Park at the beginning of the 2001/02 season, but had managed to avoid being called upon in that capacity – good job, really, since he had never played in goal in his career before, even in training sessions. The manager who signed him, Paul Sturrock, simply had a hunch that Hodges would be able to do the job (possibly because of his extreme versatility elsewhere on the pitch) and was unconcerned by the lack of any available evidence. Over the seasons, it became accepted by the players, subsequent managers, and even the Argyle fans, that Hodges would be a reliable pair of hands in a goalkeeping emergency. However, it was not until March 11th, 2008, when Sturrock was back at Home Park for his second spell as manager, that the moment to test the by now well-established theory arrived. When McCormick was dismissed for handling the ball outside his area, the gloves were passed to Hodges. Not for the first time did one of Sturrock's off-the-wall theories prove to be correct as Hodges capably kept a clean sheet for the 25 minutes that he was between the posts. The Pilgrims, however, were already behind to Ian Morris's goal and lost the match 1-0.

HE'S HERE, HE'S THERE...

LEE Hodges' stint as an emergency goalkeeper in the Pilgrims' 1-0 defeat at Scunthorpe during the 2007/08 Championship season meant that the versatile player had represented Argyle in every position. He first played for the club as a young striker in a seven-game Barclays Second Division loan spell from Tottenham Hotspur in 1993, scoring twice, but had become an established midfielder by the time he rejoined the Pilgrims from Reading in 2001, one game into their Nationwide Third Division title-winning season. In seven years and 215 games at Home Park, during which time he also helped Argyle win the Nationwide Second Division title, he was employed in every defensive and midfield position, before donning the gloves to good effect at Glanford Park.

WESTENDERS

THE Argyle line-up in the Ken Brown (senior) management era often caused confusion at away grounds, with some TV soap opera fans among the attendant journalists and supporters subconsciously reckoning that the Pilgrims were fielding only a ten-man team. The source of the confusion was right-back Ken Brown junior's name being announced over the Public Address system immediately after that of goalkeeper Rhys Wilmot. 'Wilmot, Brown...' merely conjured up, to some, an image of (James) Wilmott-Brown, a rather nasty fictional character in the soap opera *EastEnders*, played with villainous intent by William Boyde. Life would have been even more confusing if manager Brown had succeeded in a bid to buy Peter Weir from Leicester City and play him up front alongside Tommy Tynan.

LIKE FATHER...

THE Browns continued a long and proud tradition of Argyle managers enjoying a professional, as well as personal, relationship with their offspring that both preceded and succeeded them. The nepotistic line stretches all the way back to William Fullerton, who was manager of the Pilgrims for one Southern League season, 1906/07, and who selected his male offspring for 15 games of that campaign. Bob Jack, the Pilgrims' first Football League manager, continued the familial familiarity. Bob, who was Argyle manager for 29 of the 34 seasons between 1905 and 1938, picked his number one son David (or 'David Bone Nightingale' to give him his luxurious full name) 48 times. That earned David a big-money move (i.e. £3,500) to Bolton Wanderers, where he went on to fame – as the first person to score at Wembley, for Bolton against West Ham United in the 1923 White Horse Final in which future Argyle manager Jack Tresadern played for West Ham – and fortune, as the first player in the world to be transferred for a five-figure sum (Bolton Wanderers to Arsenal, 1928, £10,890, a bargain price obtained by Arsenal manager Herbert Chapman, who surreptitiously allowed the Bolton negotiators to get soused – and, consequently, more amenable – while he sipped ginless gin and tonics). Two years after David trotted off to Bolton, Bob blooded number two son, Rollo, who followed big bro to Bolton for £1,500 after just 17 games for the Pilgrims. A third son, Donald, failed to complete a Jack sibling hat-trick at Home Park but did join the family dynasty at Burnden Park.

...LIKE SON

AS well as the Jacks and Browns (not to be confused with American singer-songwriter Jackson Browne, who is obviously a Newcastle United fan, judging by the track Black & White on his Lives In The Balance album), Argyle have had four other father-son manager-player combos. In December 1994, Peter Shilton (manager 1992-95) gave son Sam (4 appearances, 0 goals, 1994-95) his debut in a 2-1 FA Cup second-round victory over AFC Bournemouth; just over seven years later, Paul Sturrock (manager 2000-2004, 2007-) handed number one son Blair (71 appearances, 3 goals, 2001-04) his debut in a 1-0 Nationwide Third Division victory over Darlington at Home Park, in which substitute Blair laid on David Friio's deciding goal. Sturrock's long-time assistant, Kevin Summerfield, was caretaker-manager of the Pilgrims before and after Sturrock (2000, 2004) and his son Luke (69 appearances, 4 goals, 2005-09) made it through the Argyle ranks to earn a debut under Bobby Williamson against Leicester in the final game of the 2004-05 Championship season. Anthony Pulis, son of (you've guessed it) Tony Pulis, made five substitute appearances on loan from his dad's former (and future) club, Stoke City in the 2005-06 Championship, his debut coming on April Fool's Day in a 2-0 win over Wolves at Home Park.

FAMILY TIES

THE Jacks, Shiltons and Summerfields have something else in common. They also represented two generations of the same family to have played for the Pilgrims. Outside-left Bob Jack made 101 appearances between 1903-1906, and one more in 1910 when he returned to Home Park; Kevin Summerfield represented the Greens 162 times between 1984-90; and Peter Shilton was player-manager (his only managerial appointment following his illustrious playing career) on 43 occasions between 1992-95. One further pairing to play the Argyle generation game was the Swiggs. Who? Well, if they were not as well known nationally as the above, there are many Cornish football followers who would be able to tell you plenty about Bob and his son Bradley, who were big cheeses on the local scene, despite failing to cut the mustard at Home Park. Bob made three first-team appearances for the Greens between 1955 and 1957 while Bradley played four times, 27 years later. However, since two of Bradley's games were as a substitute, it is unclear who held the bragging rights in the Swiggs household.

HERE COMES THE JUDGE

ANTHONY Pulis was one of 18 players whose entire Argyle career consisted of substitute appearances. Top of the Pilgrim judges (Judge. Bench. Geddit?) was Steven Milne, a Bobby Williamson signing from Dundee in the summer of 2004, who played 13 times for the Pilgrims as a replacement striker in the subsequent Championship season, all after starting among the replacements. Nicknamed 'Savo' by his team-mates after a passing resemblance to Serbian striker Savo Milošević (that's in looks, not ability), Milne then returned to Scotland where he resumed a fairly prolific career, the high point of which was scoring both goals in St Johnstone's 2-0 November 2006 League Cup win over Rangers at Ibrox, which put the Perth side into the semi-finals. Two and a half years later, Milne scored another two goals as St Johnstone beat Morton 3-1 to win promotion to the Scottish Premier League after a seven-year absence. At the other end of the scale, eight players are in the exclusive club of players whose entire Pilgrims career has consisted of just one substitute outing. The last of these was Ryan Trudgian, who had his 12 minutes of fame in a 0-0 home draw against Rochdale on the final day of the 2000/01 Nationwide Third Division season. On the same day, defender Paul Connolly and goalkeeper Luke McCormick debuted, the pair going on to make 334 appearances between them.

ENTIRE ARGYLE CAREER AS SUBSTITUTE

The following Argyle players only ever appeared in the first team as a substitute. While a further eight players have made just one sub appearance.

Stephen Milne	2004-05	13 games
Kevin Nancekivell	2000-01	7 games
Mark Damerell	1989-91	6 games
Anthony Pulis	2005	5 games
Chris Zebroski	2004-06	5 games
Dave Cooper	1991	3 games
Dominic Richardson	1994-97	3 games
Stewart Yetton	2001-05	3 games
Paul Bannon	1984	2 games
Brendon McGovern	1998-2000	2 games

ALL IN THE FAMILY

WHEN midfielder Sam Shilton followed his FA Cup debut as a substitute in December 1994 by winning a first start the following week against Brighton & Hove Albion at Home Park, he became the youngest Argyle league debutant at 16 years and 141 days, beating the record previously held by goalkeeper James Dungey by 116 days. What made the occasion even more special (or, at least special until Argyle lost the Endsleigh Second Division game 3-0) was that young Sam was handed his moment in history by another record-holder, dad Peter, who, two and a half years earlier, had become Argyle's oldest debutant, aged 42 years and 199 days. Sam's record lasted less than two years before it was overtaken (undertaken?) by striker Lee Phillips, who, at 16 years and 43 days, had, in the great tradition of events such as these, to obtain permission from his school's headmaster (has anyone ever said 'no' to such a request?) before playing the last two minutes of a 2-0 Nationwide Second Division win over Gillingham on October 29th, 1996.

UPTON LEFT

ARGYLE'S youngest ever goalscorer is another 16-year-old substitute. Darren Bastow was precisely 16 years and 316 days on 3 November, 1998, when he scored in the 85th minute of the Pilgrims' 3-0 Nationwide Third Division victory over Brentford at Home Park. Nine more appearances followed before Darren was upgraded from trainee to professional on his 17th birthday. A year after his amazing debut, he was trialled by top-flight sides Derby County and Wimbledon and seemed to have the football world at his talented young feet. Bizarrely, after 53 games and four goals, he suddenly turned his back on the professional game in favour of playing for South Devon League side Upton Athletic, then managed by his father, alongside brothers Alex and Paul and his cousin, Ian Bastow, a former Torquay United player. "I just did not want to play football anymore," Darren later explained. "It had nothing to do with Plymouth – they are a great club and were always good to me – but I just got fed up with it all. Maybe I should have stuck at it; maybe my age had something to do with it. I was too young to realise what I was throwing away. It was purely a football reason, though."

BIG-HEARTED

JAMES Dungey was one of the smallest Argyle goalkeepers, but not the smallest. That honour is shared between Peter Dyer, who played eight games in the Second Division and Third Division (South) between 1955 and 1957, and George McKenzie, who played in one Second Division match in the 1934/35 season. Both men were 5ft 7ins.

TEENAGE KICKS

OTHER Argyle young 'uns include: Colin Sullivan, aged 16 years and 269 days when he played at left-back at home to Rotherham United in a Second Division game on March 19th, 1968: Argyle lost 1-0; Dan Gosling, aged 16 years and 311 days when he came on as substitute and played in midfield in a 1-0 home Championship victory against Hull City on December 9th, 2006; and Richard Reynolds, aged 16 years and 336 days when he played as a striker in a 2-2 Second Division draw away to Ipswich on January 16th, 1965.

FATHER TIME

PETER Shilton remains the oldest person to have ever pulled on an Argyle shirt. At the time of his last game – a 4-2 Endsleigh Second Division defeat at Burnley on October 9th, 1993 – he was 44 years and 21 days, easily older than the comparatively sprightly John Oakes had been on his final Argyle appearance on the last day of the 1947-48 Second Division season, a 2-2 home draw with Bradford Park Avenue. Centre-back Oakes played just that one season after joining from Charlton. His debut – aged 41 years and 344 days – was a 6-1 Second Division defeat at Newcastle. In comparison, Shilton kept a clean sheet on his debut, a 0-0 Barclay's League Second Division draw against Charlton Athletic at West Ham's Upton Park.

THE TERMINATOR

PETER Shilton was never sacked as manager. Due to legal niceties, he was suspended from his duties. Then, a week after the suspension was announced, Shilton terminated his own employment. "[Argyle] have broken his contract and therefore he has terminated his employment in response to their breach of contract," said his solicitor, Mike Morrison.

LEFT FOOT

FORTY-SOMETHING Pilgrims Peter Shilton and John Oakes were spring lambs compared to the oldest person to be registered with the Football League as an Argyle squad member. That honour goes to the Rt. Hon. Michael Foot, who toasted his 90th birthday in the same season as the Pilgrims celebrated their own 100th birthday – 2003/04. Michael, a lifelong Argyle fan, was a director of the club at the time and was handed the number 90 shirt as a very personal gift. The talented veteran left-winger (that's as in politics, not football) who was Labour Party leader between 1990 and 1993 was formally unveiled as a player at a Home Park ceremony on the eve of the Pilgrims' Nationwide Second Division season-opener against Grimsby Town. Michael, the son of Isaac Foot, a solicitor and founder of a Plymouth law firm, was born in Plymouth in 1913, and was educated at Plymouth College Prep School. He later lived in Hampstead, in Pilgrims Lane… not coincidentally. The road was originally Worsley Road before Michael led a campaign to get it changed and he later said: "We named it after the famous Pilgrims. It is the best name for a football team and it seemed like the best name for a street, too. We had to get the consent from everyone in the street to change it – but there was no objection."

HEAD CASE

RAY Prosser, a qualified referee, was appointed Argyle's referee liaison officer in 1997. If any of the four FA-appointed officials are unable to take part, the matchday referee can request the referee liaison officer to take over the duties of the fourth official, and Ray was required to fulfil the fourth official's duties during his first full season in November 1997, an FA Cup tie against Cambridge United which finished 0-0. Cambridge were about to bring on a substitute, their all-time leading goalscorer, John Taylor, in place of Michael Kyd, so Ray duly took charge of the substitutes' board and lifted it to show Taylor's number. As he turned to show the board to another area of the crowd, he accidentally caught Taylor in the eye with the board. Taylor had to receive treatment but was all right, although the Cambridge bench was not amused. Taylor survived to go on and become Cambridge United's oldest player, and was their manager for four seasons.

PETER SHILTON: GOLDEN OLDIE

NO SUBSTITUTE

LIKE Sam Shilton and Darren Bastow – to name but two – Blair Sturrock made his debut as a substitute. In fact, he made by far the majority of his Argyle appearances as a substitute. Out of the 71 times he appeared for the Greens, 60 of them were from the bench – a staggering 84.5% of his Argyle career. If ever there was a player who was used to replace a tiring striker rather like baseball teams use a reserve pitcher, it was Blair: if the team needed a goal, he was sent on by his dad to get one; if they were winning, he was sent on to retain possession and was a master exponent in the dark art of taking the ball into a corner and holding it there while opposition players hacked away at his ankles. His team-mates knew precisely his role and loved him for his ability to carry it out to perfection. Sturrock junior's team-mate and fellow striker Nathan Lowndes was another player to come on from the bench for more than 50% of his Pilgrims appearances, while a third forward from the same era, Marino Keith was also a Sturrock supersub. In fact, of the top ten top subbies, half of them played under Luggy in either his first or second spell as Argyle manager. Makes you wonder who actually started games up front under the Scot.

Most Substitute Appearances By Percentage

Player		Apps	Starts	Subs	
Blair Sturrock	2001-2004	71	11	60	84.51%
Martin Gritton	1998-2002	55	20	35	63.64%
Lee Phillips	1996-2001	61	25	36	59.02%
Nathan Lowndes	2002-2004	59	29	30	50.85%
Marc Edworthy	1991-1995	97	32	65	67.01%
Rory Fallon	2007-2009	93	46	47	50.54%
Marino Keith	2001-2005	131	76	55	41.98%
Earl Jean	1997-1999	76	47	29	38.16%
Nick Chadwick	2005-2008	83	53	30	36.14%
Ákos Buzsáky	2005-2008	106	74	32	30.19%

(criteria of twenty or more Argyle appearances)

MORE PROSAICALLY

SIXTEEN players with the surname Smith have played for Argyle, the most recent being Dan Smith, a Cornish winger who made two substitute appearances in the 2007-08 Championship season.

I NAME THIS CHILD...

AH yes, Marino Keith – or 'Dan', as he was inevitably known in the Argyle dressing-room – the Scot given an Italian name by his French grandmother. An exotic name, of which there have been more than a few at Home Park. Jimmy Cherrie Crawford, anyone? Or how about Robinson Gourlay Nicholl Wyllie? Or this lot: Patrick Kwame Ampadu, Septimus Atterbury, Barrington Belgrave, David Gort Burnside, Francis James Augustus Cassidy, Giancarlo Michele Corazzin, Cornelius Dougall, Richard Garfield Flash, Clevere Forde, Ronald Carlton Maugé, Morton Meredith Morgan, Anthony Eldred Rounsvell, Danis Mahmut Mehmet Salman, John Youngman Thomson, Johannes Christison Van Rossum, and Barry Emmanuel Vassallo.

THE BIGGER THEY ARE...

FORGET Kaka or Ronaldinho – Argyle once had the biggest name in football. Forbes Phillipson-Masters, a central defender who made 137 appearances between 1979-82, was, in his time, the longest name to be registered with the Football League. It used to be said that the most unpopular man on the Pilgrims terraces was the one who started the chant "Give us an F..." However, when the chant went its full distance, it did include the rather surreal exhortation to "Give us a hyphen".

LESS IS MORE

AT the other end of the scale to Forbes etc. (23 letters and one hyphen) was Tony Obi (5 Canon Third Division appearances in 1985) who, with 7 letters in his entire name, is the shortest-named player to have represented the Greens. Someone with far too much time on their hands once calculated that, if they both wrote at the same speed, Tony could have signed three times as many autographs as Forbes.

FIRST PICKS

DOWN the years, the Pilgrims have had a Steve CHERRY, a Richard and a Jimmy LOGAN, a Geoff PEACH, and a Calvin PLUMmer – all plucked from other clubs, naturally.

GETTING THE BIRD

THE fruity crowd on the previous page would obviously have had to keep an eye out for Tony BIRD, Jack COCK, Dean CROWE, Phil KITE, Scott PARTRIDGE, Alan PEACOCK, Peter SWAN and Dan GOSLING.

BULLEY FOR HIM

ARGYLE once fielded a player who, it could be argued, was born to be a Pilgrim. Dan Bulley, a striker on the club's books at the beginning of the 21st century, never quite made it to the first-team ranks, which is a shame because his dad Stuart was such a fan of the Greens that he had given his eldest the middle name 'Argyle'. Dan later carved out a significant career in America that included representing Great Britain at the 2007 World University Games.

EASTER TIME

IN 2008, Easter Day was on March 23rd. Twenty-four hours earlier, the Pilgrims had entertained Watford in a Championship game at Home Park. The game ended 1-1. Argyle's goalscorer was Jermaine… Easter.

THEY SHOULD WRITE A BOOK ABOUT…

TOMMY Tynan. In fact, they have. Twice. A 1990 effort by a person not unrelated to one of the authors of this book called *Tommy: A Life at the Soccer Factory* and, proving the enduring nature of the subject, a 2009 update called *The Original Football Idol*, by Ryan Danes. Without giving away too much of the contents of either, Tommy had already won a newspaper competition to join Bill Shankly's Liverpool and been a headline-grabbing goalscorer at Sheffield Wednesday, Lincoln City and Newport County (who he helped to the quarter-finals of the European Cup-Winners' Cup) before he arrived at Home Park in 1983. A key member of Johnny Hore's FA Cup semi-finalists that campaign, he topped that with 32 goals the following season. However, it was not until Tommy left the Pilgrims and returned at the end of the 1985-86 season that his Argyle legend was born. Tommy scored 10 goals in the run-in of that Canon Third Division campaign to help earn Argyle promotion, and effectively begin a second, four-year stint at Home Park which ended after he had worn the green 310 times, scoring 144 goals.

PURE GOALS

TOMMY Tynan was leading goalscorer for Argyle in each of the six full seasons that he played for the club (and still made double-figures in 1985/86, when he played just nine times). The 31 goals he scored for the Pilgrims in the 1984/85 Canon Third Division season made him the country's leading league goalscorer, jointly with future Pilgrims team-mate John Clayton, then of Tranmere Rovers. Tynan's Argyle league goals: 1983/84: 12; 1984/85: 31; 1985/86: 10; 1986/87: 18; 1987/88: 16; 1988/89: 24; 1989/90: 15.

BLACK MARK

TOMMY Tynan ranks third in the list of Argyle's all-time top goalscorers, just behind Wilf Carter but a long way from the 184-goal mark set by Sammy Black between 1924 and 1938. Black, 5ft 6ins, size four feet, and nicknamed the Mighty Atom, arrived at Home Park from Scottish side Kirkintilloch Rob Roy. When Argyle toured South America in 1924, manager Robert Jack went with them but asked Pilgrims secretary Louis Crabbe to find some players. After a trip to Scotland, Crabbe signed three players: "There is J. Macmillan, of Arbroath, a right-winger; R. Wallace, an inside-forward, of Hamilton Accies; and S. Black, an outside-left, from Kirkintilloch Rob Roy. The last named is a regular box of tricks, and will soon be challenging for a permanent place in the chief side." Macmillan never played for the Pilgrims; Wallace played once then went to Torquay; and Black set out on the path to a record which will never be broken.

STARTING OUT

FOR some reason, lots of Argyle players have made their first-team debut against Bury, including Kevin Hodges, in an away Third Division game on 12 September 1978 – who, at that time, would have expected the teenage defender to go on and break the Argyle appearance record? Kevin had only just turned 18 when Malcolm Allison, in his second stint as Pilgrims' manager, called him up to replace the injured Brian Bason for the first of his 600-plus appearances in the green. Alan Banks, Kevin Blackwell, Tommy Black, Keith Etheridge, Reg Gibson, Mark Graves, Neil Hards, Bill Harper, Nicky Jennings, Barrie Meyer, Forbes Phillipson-Masters and John 'Cardiff' Williams also all made their debut against Bury.

THREE TIMES A FAVOURITE

NOT surprisingly, Tommy Tynan, adored by the Green Army, was voted Player of the Season on three occasions, and is the only player to have won that award more than twice. The five two-time winners are: Paul Mariner, George Foster, Steve McCall, Mick Heathcote and Paul Wotton.

ARGYLE PLAYER OF THE SEASON

Season	Player	Season	Player
1965/66	Johnny Newman	1987/88	Steve Cherry
1966/67	Norman Piper	1988/89	Tommy Tynan
1967/68	Pat Dunne	1989/90	Nicky Marker
1968/69	David Burnside	1990/91	Kenny Brown
1969/70	Derek Rickard	1991/92	Dwight Marshall
1970/71	Jim Furnell	1992/93	Steve McCall
1971/72	Dave Provan	1993/94	Steve McCall
1972/73	Neil Hague	1994/95	Marc Edworthy
1973/74	Ernie Machin	1995/96	Mick Heathcote
1974/75	Paul Mariner	1996/97	Chris Billy
1975/76	Paul Mariner	1997/98	Martin Barlow / Carlo Corazzin
1976/77	Neil Ramsbottom	1998/99	Mick Heathcote
1977/78	George Foster	1999/00	Paul McGregor
1978/79	Fred Binney	2000/01	Wayne O'Sullivan
1979/80	George Foster	2001/02	Graham Coughlan
1980/81	David Kemp	2002/03	Paul Wotton
1981/82	John Sims	2003/04	Mickey Evans
1982/83	Gordon Nisbet	2004/05	Paul Wotton
1983/84	Gordon Staniforth	2005/06	David Norris
1984/85	Tommy Tynan	2006/07	Lilian Nalis
1985/86	Kevin Hodges	2007/08	Krisztián Timár
1986/87	Tommy Tynan	2008/09	Romain Larrieu

GROUNDSMAN WILLIE

ARGYLE'S first groundsman was William Tomlinson, who was appointed in 1901. His family had a plant nursery in the city, and his son continued working in the Argyle office until the 1950s.

BEST EVER

DESPITE competition from the likes of Billy Rafferty, Jack Cock, Maurice Tadman, Wilf Carter, Jack Leslie, Jack Vidler, and Ryan Trudgian, Tommy Tynan was named as one of the two strikers in the Pilgrims' Team of the Century, as voted for by the club's fans in the Greens' Centenary Season of 2003/04. His partner was Paul Mariner and the two spearheaded a team, unveiled at the club's Centenary Ball in Plymouth Guildhall in 2004, comprising: 1, Jim Furnell, 2, Gordon Nisbet, 3, Colin Sullivan, 4, Johnny Williams, 5, Jack Chisholm, 6, Graham Coughlan, 7, Kevin Hodges, 8, Ernie Machin, 9, Tommy Tynan, 10, Paul Mariner, 11, Sammy Black/Garry Nelson. The manager was Paul Sturrock, whose number six was the only contemporaneous player among the selections.

AND WOTTSY MAKES 14

THE Team of the Century, and its manager, were also later named as the first inductees into the Pilgrims' Hall of Fame. Towards the end of the 2008/09 season, Argyle held a vote to choose the next Hall of Famer, and the Green Army plumped for Paul Wotton, twice captain of an Argyle promotion-winning side and centre-back partner in the 2001/02 Nationwide Third Division championship side of fellow inductee Graham Coughlan.

CHEERS TOMMY

IN the days before the media offered an easy post-playing career, the pub trade was always popular. Tommy Tynan followed a veritable list of Argyle greats in becoming mine host of a licensed premises, in his case of the Golden Hind, a few goal kicks from Home Park. Indeed, one of his predecessors behind the pumps had been ex-Argyle custodian, the appropriately named Bill Shortt. Other former Pilgrims who polished the optics and flushed through the pipes on a regular basis were: Jack Chisholm (The Pennycomequick), Pat Glover (Kings Arms, Tamerton Foliot), Archie Gorman (The Blue Monkey and George Hotel, Buckfastleigh), Alex Govan (Hyde Park), Moses Russell (The Talbot), Bill Shortt (The Golden Hind and The Duke Of York, Tavistock), Billy Strauss (The Tandem and The Standard), Freddie Titmuss (The Cherry Tree and Laira Hotel), Tommy Tynan (The Golden Hind and The Stoke Social Club) and Harry Wilcox (The Nottingham).

HELLO, GOODBYE

NOT all the Argyle records Tommy Tynan holds are ones to be beaten. Among his personal bests (or, in this case, personal worsts) is one for the quickest sending-offs of an Argyle player at Home Park. Tynan walked in the third minute after spitting at Alan Walker, of Lincoln City, in a Canon Third Division game in January 1984. Walker later played twice for the Pilgrims on loan from Gillingham, scoring a goal, in the 1992/93 Barclays Third Division campaign, by which time Tommy was well out of gobbing range. The match ended 2-2, or 10-11, depending on what you were counting.

MAT RED

TOMMY Tynan's walk to the dressing-room after only three minutes was positively tardy compared to the all-time Argyle fastest sending-off, 'achieved' by Mathais Kouo-Doumbe in a Championship game at Ipswich in March 2007. The French defender was dismissed by referee Jonathan Moss after the official had firstly explicitly waved away muted home cries for a foul after Mat and Jon Walters clashed shoulder to shoulder on the edge of the Argyle penalty area. Moss was persuaded to change his mind, and dismiss Doumbe, by linesman Steve Rubery, who had been twice as far away from the incident than Moss and viewed it from a far worse angle. Argyle's ten men lost 3-0. "There was small contact between us, but nothing special," said the centre-back. "The referee said nothing, acted like it was nothing at all, but the linesman apparently saw something and asked him to go and see him. He just decided it was a red card. He didn't say anything. I was speechless. I couldn't believe it."

SUNDAY WORST

AT least they finished with ten men. Thirty-three years to the month earlier at Vale Park, the Wembley of the North, the Pilgrims had created Football League history by having three men sent off in the same Third Division game, on March 10th, 1974. Steve Davey was shown to the proverbial early bath by referee Kevin McNally in the first half, with Dave Provan and Bobby Saxton following in injury time. Argyle lost 2-1 in what was their first ever Sunday league game. And a Sunday League performance to match.

OFF, OFF, OFF

ON February 22nd, 1997, the Pilgrims again ended a game with only eight men. Despite the disadvantage, they won a Nationwide Second Division match 2-1 at Chesterfield, but that might have been because the home side were reduced to nine men after having two players dismissed themselves. Argyle midfielder Ronnie Maugé was first to see red in what became dubbed the Battle of Saltergate, with two players from each side – Argyle's Richard Logan and Tony James, and Chesterfield's Kevin Davies and Darren Carr – later dismissed following a 21-man brawl. Even then, Ronnie was on his feet in the stand wanting to get involved. Bless him. On a bygones are bygones basis, Carr later joined the Pilgrims for a pre-season trial but, despite being given a fighting chance to earn a contract, did not progress further.

FOLLOWING THROUGH

CURIOUSLY, in each of the three seasons, from 2006/07 to 2008/09, Argyle had an instance of one red card following another within less than two weeks. Barry Hayles was dismissed in a home game against Southampton on New Year's Day, to be followed by Paul Connolly five days later in an FA Cup tie at Peterborough. In March 2008, Pilgrims' goalkeeper Luke McCormick saw red in a Championship game at Scunthorpe, 11 days before Hungarian winger Péter Halmosi was sent off (while on a stretcher, bizarrely) in a home league game against Watford. On December 20th 2008, Simon Walton saw in Christmas with a three-match suspension after being given his marching orders at Barnsley: eight days later, David McNamee saw red, which ruled him out of a glamour FA Cup tie at Arsenal, when he committed a professional foul on Cardiff striker Michael Chopra at Ninian Park. Argyle failed to win any of the games in which they were numerically disadvantaged.

YELLOW PERIL

THE quickest booking received by a player at Home Park went to homecoming Pilgrim Micky Horswill in a Third Division game on April 7th, 1979. In the amber and black of Hull, Mick the Quick saw yellow for fouling Gary Megson after seven seconds. Horswill, who made more than 100 appearances for the Greens between 1975-78, might have lost his head, but Argyle lost the game, 4-3.

SPARKES OF CONTROVERSY

RAY Sparkes also saw yellow on his first visit to Home Park in April 1979 when Argyle played Gillingham on the 21st of the month. Ray, from Plymouth, attended the match as a spectator with his son Craig, and became the centre of attention after ten minutes, when a linesman started waving his flag to get referee Bill Bombroff's attention. The assistant pointed across the pitch towards Ray, and, following a discussion, Ray was asked to move. The bright yellow jacket that Ray was wearing clashed with the Gillingham players' shirts, making it difficult for the linesman to judge offsides. Ray thought he had a good seat, so, rather than move, he decided to remove his jacket. Argyle, who were just below halfway in the Third Division table, beat Gillingham 2-1 but eventually missed out on promotion by two points.

HORE GREEN AT THE VALLEY

THE first player to be used as a substitute for Argyle was Johnny Hore, who came on for the injured Frank Lord in a Second Division game against Charlton Athletic at the Valley on August 31st, 1965. The game ended 1-1, with Mike Trebilcock scoring for the Pilgrims. On the opening day of the season – the first in which substitutes were permitted (for injured players only) – John was due to be the Pilgrims' number 12 against Portsmouth at Fratton Park but was drafted into the first XI before the game when team-mate Johnny Newman was ruled out by a septic throat.

NO GOING BACK

GORDON Nisbet, the right-back in Argyle's Team of the Century, played more than 300 times for the Pilgrims between 1980 and 1987, and was Player of the Season in 1982/83. It is a well-known piece of trivia that Nizzie began his professional career as a goalkeeper, with top-flight West Bromwich Albion, at the age of just 18. He converted to right-back soon afterwards and limited his custodian duties to emergencies, such as the 1986 New Year's Day Canon Third Division draw with Cardiff at Home Park, when goalkeeper Geoff Crudgington suffered a blow to the head. With Argyle conceding four goals in a 4-4 draw, Nizzie proved beyond a shadow of a doubt that he had made the right career choice as a teenager at the Hawthorns.

MAKING HIS MARK

ONE of the high points of Argyle's 2003/04 Centenary Season was the Parade of Pilgrims before the 0-0 home Nationwide Third Division draw with Wrexham on March 27th – 100 former players and one current French goalkeeper went on a lap of honour, including the oldest Pilgrim on parade, 89-year-old Marcus Murphy. After being introduced to the crowd, it was suggested to Marcus that he might like to take a short cut to the finish. He turned on his heels... and ran the length of the Lyndhurst side. The sight of several press photographers struggling to keep up with the sprightly octogenarian was an enduring memory of a fine day. The 100 players, who totalled 10,806 first-team starting league appearances, were: Peter Anderson 241, Dougie Anderson 17, Gordon Astall 188, Terry Austin 58, George Baker 78, Peta Balać 40, Geoff Banton 6, Geoff Barnsley 131, Tommy Barrett 26, Jon Beswetherick 133, Mike Bickle 171, Fred Binney 67, Stuart Brace 9, Johnny Brown 9, Kenny Brown 126, Ken Brown manager, Colin Buckingham 16, David Burnside 105, Phil Burrows 81, Adrian Burrows 272, David Byrne 52, Wilf Carter 254, Paul Chapman 2, Jeremy Collins 4, Dave Corbett 84, Geoff Crudgington 326, Peter Darke 94, Steve Davey 213, Eric Davis 63, Richard Davis 23, John Delve 127, Neil Dougall 274, Ernie Edds 85, Keith Etheridge 30, Jim Furnell 180, Alex Govan 142, Neil Hague 98, Chris Harrison 315, Martin Harvey coach, Neil Heaney 1, Martin Hodge 60, Kevin Hodges 502, John Hore 393, Mickey Horswill 98, Don Hutchins 94, Reg Jenkins 16, Nicky Jennings 98, Dennis John 3, Barrie Jones 98, Peter Langman 90, Romain Larrieu 122, Les Latcham 83, Dave Lean 44, John Leiper 75, Ernie Machin 57, Ken Maloy 62, Nicky Marker 205, John Matthews 131, Ronnie Maugé 119, Jimmy McAnearney 135, Steve McCall 125, Sean McCarthy 133, John Mitten 43, Jock Morrison 105, Marcus Murphy 15, Malcolm Musgrove coach, Duncan Neale 141, Garry Nelson 71, Gordon Nisbet 281, Bill Olver 5, John Peddelty 30, Harry Penk 104, Norman Piper 215, Billy Rafferty 89, Colin Randell 247, Mike Reeves 107, Derek Rickard 101, Dave Roberts 11, Andy Rogers 159, Tony Rounsevell 34, Mark Rowe 46, Danis Salman 71, Jon Sheffield 155, Barry Silkman 14, John Sillett 37, John Sims 161, Kevin Smart 32, Arthur Stenner 9, Kevin Summerfield 118, Bob Swiggs 3, Darren Tallon 1, Rex Tilley 123, Tommy Tynan 261, John Uzzell 292, Kenny Veysey 5, Johnny Williams 411, John L. Williams 34, George Willis 56, Rhys Wilmot 133, and Reg Wyatt 202.

A BRIEF HISTORY OF GREEN

IT was in 1886 that Argyle was founded. In those days, football was the provenance of the armed forces and public schools (indeed, the word 'soccer' is an upper-class contraction of 'association football', just as 'rugger' was a condensed slang from 'rugby football') and the two came together rather neatly in the formation of 'Argyle FC' – NB. not 'Plymouth Argyle'. Frank Howard Grose and William Pethybridge were two former pupils of Dunheved College, Launceston, who fancied starting their own team. Like you do. So they did, following, it is fabled, a meeting in the Borough Arms coffee house in Bedford Street, Plymouth. Depending on which theory you subscribe to, the new team was named (a) in honour of the Argyll & Sutherland Highlanders regiment, the reigning Army champions who were based in the city; (b) after Argyll Terrace, in which Grose and Pethybridge were lodging; or (c) both of the above. Given that Argyle FC's colours were precisely the same as the green, black and white tartan of the Argyll & Sutherlands, it seems that either (a) or (c) is correct.

GREEN SHOOTS

WHEN and why 'Argyll' mutated into 'Argyle' is not known, but it seems likely there was a misreading of a loopy letter 'e' somewhere along the line. Whatever, Argyle FC's first recorded game was played on Saturday, October 9th, 1886 at Dunheved College, Launceston, the alma mater of Grose and Pethybridge. The new side, captained by Grose, lost 2-0. In those days, the club's training ground was at Freedom Fields and a first reference to a home pitch is not found until December, when they lined up against the area's premier team, Plymouth United (one of the first teams in the world to use the suffix 'United', if not the first) at 'the Argyle Ground' in the Mount Gould area of Plymouth. In 1887, they managed to get a home pitch at Tothill, at what is known today as Astor Field. From 1889, they played home games at Marsh Mills, now very much part of the city and home to a splendid flyover and the Sainsbury's with the wimples, but then an area so far out of town that trains were laid on to take spectators to the match. In 1899/1900, the Argyle (Association) Football Club won its first championship, the Devon Senior League.

ARGYLE FC'S FIRST FIVE OPPONENTS

Dunheved College, Launceston
Caxtons
Plymouth College
Royal Artillery
Tavistock Grammar School

OUT WITH THE OLD...

IN 1894, eight years after Grose and Pethybridge ordered a coffee and ended up with a football club, Argyle FC went bust. Results, as ever, played the largest part in their ceasing to exist. However, after three years, the name was back in the public consciousness thanks to one Clarence Newby Spooner. Spooner was a well-known businessman in the town, with the Spooner & Co. Department Store bearing his family name. Clarence took upon himself the presidency of the Argyle Football Club, expanding it into the Argyle Athletic Club, which encompassed a number of sports and pastimes. With brothers Guy, John and Stanley alongside him on the board, he masterminded the drive into the professional era. In 1900, Argyle moved into a field with a couple of unprepossessing stands called Home Park, after which they turned professional, and entered the Southern and Western Leagues, although their membership of the former was dependent on them paying the expenses of their visitors.

BOOTED OUT

PLYMOUTH Argyle were not the first occupants of Home Park. Devonport Rugby Club were tenants until the eve of the 20th century when they vacated the premises in a dispute over the rent. Great move, lads. One of the first recorded games of football (non egg-chasing variety) happened in May 1887, when the Ladies Reds beat the Ladies Blues 1-0. At least, I think it was football. According to an 1881 map, there was no football ground called Home Park. At that time, Plymouth was a town, and Milehouse, the area of Plymouth in which the Pilgrims play, was named, with blinding logic, after a house a mile away from the Blockhouse in Devonport. The area to the east was the 'out lands' of the town, hence Outland Road, which is where Home Park is today.

HOME, SWEET HOME

HOME Park was built, and named, in 1893 at a cost of £8,000, which was raised from £1 shares. Good job no-one had thought of naming rights back in those days, otherwise Argyle might today be playing in the Spooner Stadium. Central Park, the area surrounding Home Park now, did not exist until 1931. Home Park was called 'the Home Park Recreation Ground' and was then on the outskirts of the town. The approaches were through Pennycomequick (that's a place, not an exhortation), past fields and farms, and there was a stile to climb over. If coming from the famous Stonehouse or Devonport towns, there was a pathfield past an old burial ground and another stile, which survived until 1953. Inside the ground, there were no terraces, toilets or crush barriers; three sides of the ground were slag heaps; and the stand was a wooden one about 40 yards long with a gable roof. There was an asphalt running track around the pitch which the Argyle Athletic Club used.

A PONY ON IT

AFTER the Argyle Athletic Club moved into the Home Park Recreation Ground in 1901, more established football sides like Aston Villa, Notts County and Sheffield Wednesday played there in exhibition games, the five-figure crowds they attracted helping to boost the Pilgrims' attempts to become Southern League members. As well as football, the Park was home to such diverse distractions as bicycle-racing, pony-trotting and whippet-racing. Not at the same time, although I would have paid good money to see the Chris Hoy of his day taking on a whippet. The first event held at the ground was an athletics meeting, which makes sense. In 1903, the football club rented the ground from the Athletic Club.

HEROES AND VILLANS

THE first professional football club to play Argyle at Home Park was Aston Villa, who won 7-0 in a friendly match between the two clubs. The exact date of the friendly is unknown, but it took place between January 1st and April 24th, 1903.

TIMBER...

IN 1930, the wooden stand that had stood since the Pilgrims had moved into Home Park, was pulled down and replaced by a larger and more modern structure with changing-rooms and offices. The Supporters' Club paid £1,500 towards the roof cost and Argyle got some money from a sale of the timber from the old stand. The cost of this new stand was £11,000. At the same time, the other three sides of the ground were built up with concrete terracing and crush barriers. There was a rope all the way around the pitch, no fence, and the corners were made up with railway sleepers. And you try and tell the young people of today that... they won't believe you.

HOME PARKING

ALSO in 1930, as well as extensive renovation work for the Pilgrims' first season in the Second Division, the large club car park on Outland Road, which remains there to this day, was opened. It was used for the first time on August 30th, 1930, the opening day of the season, when Argyle played Everton – one of only three times the Toffeemen have visited Home Park for a league game. They would still recognise the car park, though.

FRONTING UP

THE familiar front entrance of Home Park was built in 1936. Like a lot of Home Park over the years, it was paid for by the Supporters' Club.

FIRE...

ARGYLE were too hot for Aberdare Athletic in a Third Division (South) game at Home Park on September 26th, 1925, when the Welsh side was trounced 7-2. During the match, which was obviously engrossing, a fire broke out in the grandstand. No players and most supporters, obviously caught up in the blaze of goals, paid any heed to the flames – caused by a carelessly tossed still lit match – so it is a good job the incident was quickly dealt with by the swift application of a few buckets of water. Two quirks from this game: (i) Argyle's seven goals were shared by six different players; and (ii) Aberdare's Welsh international goalkeeper Arthur Brown was Man of the Match.

...I SAID 'FIRE'...

THE west wing of the Argyle grandstand was considerably damaged by a fire which broke out a few hours after a Second Division match with Tottenham Hotspur on Wednesday, March 9th, 1938. It had been smouldering for hours and was discovered by the groundsman, who heard the crackling of flames at around 10pm. Thank goodness for overtime. The fire brigade was able to confine the fire to the wing stand, and had it under control by midnight, but most of the rows of wooden terracing were damaged.

...OH PLEASE YOURSELF

ON May 3rd, 2009, just hours before the Pilgrims' Championship game with Watford at Home Park, a fire broke out in the club's laundry room. Kit man Ian Pearce, known to everyone at the football club as 'Jacko' because of an apparent likeness to movie star Jack Nicholson, smelled burning and discovered bags of players' strips on fire. He raised the alarm and tackled the blaze with a fire extinguisher, suffering slight burns to his hands. Argyle won the Tuesday night game 2-1, with Jacko on the bench.

FAT'S YOUR LOT

ARGYLE goalkeeper Geoff Crudgington knows how bad fire can be from a dreadful experience he had at his home close to Home Park, hours before a home match against Bradford City on February 19th, 1983. A pan of fat caught fire and Geoff's immediate reaction was to throw it out the back door, but, as he did so, the fat was blown back towards him and caught his sweater. The sweater quickly melted (it was the '80s – they used all manner of dubious materials in those days) and Geoff sustained second degree burns around his waist and back. He arrived at Home Park doubting whether he would play, and the club doctor was still treating him with less than an hour to go for kick-off. Reserve goalkeeper Neil Hards was already travelling to an away reserve match, so manager Bobby Moncur's only other option was to give full-back Gordon Nisbet the number one shirt. Geoff was in great pain but decided to play, despite the doctor warning that he might get an adverse reaction. He played the whole of the Third Division match, which Argyle won 3-1.

KNOCKED DOWN...

DURING the Second World War, Plymouth – an important naval city – suffered appallingly at the hands of the Luftwaffe, and Home Park was, like much of the place, flattened beyond recognition. The area under the main grandstand was used to store furniture belonging to families who had suffered earlier bombing, but, having survived one hit, their belongings were lost when Home Park was caught up in the continual blitzkriegs. The pitch at Home Park was transformed into three very large craters, while the grandstand was all but destroyed by high explosives and incendiary bombs. Only the supporting RSJs (that's rolled steel joists) and galvanised roof were left, but they were so dangerously twisted that they eventually had to be demolished. The Devonport End stand, bought by (guess who?) the Supporters' Club in 1930, stood firm right through the war as that end of the ground was spared from any enemy action, and this was the only permanent cover at Home Park after the war.

...AND BOUNCING BACK

AFTER the war ended, the club appealed to volunteers to help deal with the shrapnel, rubble and bomb craters that had replaced the pitch and grandstands. What Hitler had not destroyed had gone to help the war effort. All the turnstiles, seating and anything else made of metal, had been ripped out and melted down. Following the example of the city, Home Park rose again. When St Andrew's Church in the city was bombed, a board was put up containing but a single word – Resurgam, Latin for "I shall rise again". New chairman Sir Clifford Tozer led the Argyle revival and Home Park was gradually restored. Two old trams were brought in and occupied the area where the Chisholm Lounge later stood: one became a boardroom with a Directors' Box upstairs; the other had various uses, including that of a changing-room for a while, even if the players had to wash down in cold water as hot water was not available. The Pilgrims were ready to take part in the one-off 1945-46 Football League (South), the first season after the cessation of hostilities, but still needed the influence of retired manager Robert Jack to persuade the Football League of that fact. They finished well bottom, but, given the blitz, simply taking part was a triumph. One of the trams was still there in 1953.

BEARING UP

UP until 1951, the players used to enter the pitch, not from under the Mayflower Grandstand, but from the corner of Home Park between the Barn Park end and the grandstand. The old dug-outs were also on that corner and, after new ones were built, remained in use on matchdays to house St John Ambulance staff and stretcher-bearers.

FINISHING OFF

IN the 1950s, designers Archibald Leitch constructed the Mayflower Grandstand at Home Park, which was still standing more than 50 years later. So too was the Chisholm Lounge in the corner of the ground between the grandstand and the Barn Park end. It is named after Jack Chisholm, a big centre-half signed from Sheffield United in 1949, and who later became captain, leading the club to promotion to the Second Division in 1952.

GOVERNMENT SAY 'NO'

UNTIL 1952, the only covered section of Home Park was the Devonport end. In 1948, Argyle wanted to build a 2,500-seat grandstand at a cost of £20,000, but the Minister of Works refused permission because at that time he could only approve work designed to prevent danger to the public, the definition of 'danger' obviously did not extend to fans exposing themselves to pneumonia or frostbite. In 1951, work started on a new Archibald Leitch 2,588-seat grandstand, and, when it was one-third completed, it was deemed safe to allow supporters to use it. Building work was completed in 1952.

LIGHTING-UP TIME

HOME Park was floodlit for the first time in 1953. The contractors for the installation were Madge & Son who had offices in Portland Square. There was a bit of mutual back-scratching; after winning the contract, Madge erected advertising boards around the floodlight pylons and advertised in the matchday programme for nearly a decade. The floodlights were officially switched on for the first time at a friendly fixture against Exeter City on October 26th 1953. It was a wet and windy evening and Argyle won 3-1 in front of a crowd of just 2,000.

JACK CHISHOLM: YOU CAN STILL HAVE A DRINK IN HIS LOUNGE

A NICE DAY OUT

IN the 1950s, local hospitals brought patients to watch Argyle's matches at Home Park. Ambulances would arrive and come in through the main entrance before disgorging their patients into a wicker basket with wheels on. This was then wheeled down the access ramp at the Barn Park corner of the ground, around to the Lyndhurst side, just a few yards from the touchline. The patients came, in all types of weather, for several years before someone realised the health and safety implications of them being hit by the ball.

TREATED LIKE ANIMALS

PLYMOUTH Zoo opened its doors behind the Barn Park end of Home Park in 1962, and remained Argyle's next-door neighbour until January 1978. In a reserve match in the early 1970s, Pilgrims midfielder Brian Johnson hit a penalty a long way over the bar at the Barn Park end and the ball was eventually recovered from the zoo's hippopotamus pen. Not by Brian, it hardly needs to be added.

HOWZAT?

IN the 1960s, Home Park played host to a number of sports other than football, notably pursuit cycling and rugby. In the late 1970s, when Kerry Packer was promoting cricket in Australia, there were plans for a night version of the game to take place at Home Park. Nothing ever came of the idea – but who knows what might happen now Twenty20 has taken off?

SOME MINOR MODIFICATIONS

PAY attention. In 1964, a roof was put over the Lyndhurst terracing; in 1967, a new players' tunnel was built under the executive boxes and Mayflower seating appeared in front of the grandstand; in 1969, the seating in the grandstand was changed to bring the combined capacity of the grandstand and the Mayflower stand up to 4,000; in 1977, the Devonport end roofing – which had survived the worst that Adolf Hitler could serve on Plymouth – was removed, as it was considered unsafe; in 1986, 16 executive boxes were installed at the rear of the Mayflower terrace seating area; and the Devonport end got its new roof in 1984 at a cost of £40,000.

TEMPORARILY PERMANENT

THE Far Post Club, a social club for Argyle supporters, was opened at Home Park in Feb, 1974. The name came from Bill Pearce, Argyle's commercial manager, who found the club in Exeter and brought it to Plymouth. The portable building was an overflow unit situated in the car park of Exeter Hospital, and it had a centre corridor with consulting rooms and offices. Watney's Brewery provided Argyle with a loan to buy the building, which was brought down the A38 on a lorry and re-sited at the Barn Park end of Home Park. The loan was repaid within two years. Club chairman Robert Daniel indicated that the lifespan of this 'temporary' building would be five years, but it is still there as I type this, 30 years after Robert's estimation for its demise.

PAISLEY PULL OVER

THE first pint to be pulled at the Far Post social club at Home Park was drawn by legendary Liverpool manager Bob Paisley, in town for John Hore's testimonial game. The club's first licence was an occasional licence, and held by a big Argyle fan Charlie 'Ginger' Casterton who, at the time, ran the Edgecombe Hotel in Millbridge. Gordon Ward was the first steward. Run by a committee until 2005, the Far Post Club was subsequently taken over by the football club.

PAY, OR NO PLAY

ON March 14th, 1973, 37,639 supporters crammed into Home Park for a sell-out friendly against Santos, the great Brazilian club side which contained not only Pele, but also Edu and Carlos Alberto. The match very nearly did not take place as, after seeing the size of the crowd, Santos wanted more money for their part in drawing the people to Home Park. Cash, please, or you are going to have to send 37,639 people away disappointed. Faced with that unhappy prospect, Argyle did what all stout men of principle would do. They paid up. Crazily, Third Division Argyle raced into a 3-0 lead, no doubt making Argyle wonder why they had bothered to shell out so much money on such poor opposition. Inevitably, though, Santos turned on the style in the second half but could not overturn Argyle's lead and lost 3-2, but with considerably heavier pockets.

CLUB OF VICE

THE Argyle Vice-Presidents' club was formed in 1969 and donated £35,000 to the Pilgrims in its first 10 years of existence. Initially, membership was limited to 100 members, but this was later increased to 150 when the lounge where they met was enlarged. Makes sense.

COTTAGE INDUSTRY

IN October 1976, Argyle bought Elm Cottage, a building adjacent to Home Park, for £20,000, as somewhere to accommodate apprentices and trialists. Another £10,000 was spent refurbishing the place and former Argyle defender, trainer and groundsman George Robertson and his wife lived there as caretakers. In 1986, Elm Cottage was sold because of financial problems at the club. It later became a veterinary surgery.

SAFETY FIRST

AS a result of the post-Hillsborough Taylor Report on Football Ground Safety published in 1990, £720,000 was earmarked for improvements to Home Park. Not all the modifications were made simply with safety in mind. Various measures for crowd control were introduced: gangways were clearly marked and kept free on match days; work was done to improve the terracing; new police surveillance facilities were installed; hospitality was improved; and changing-rooms were renovated.

JUMPERS FOR SEATS

IN 1992-93, the Lyndhurst Stand at Home Park was transformed from a terracing to an all-seated area at a cost of £60,000. The club installed 3,437 seats but not before the Pilgrims' chief executive Liz Baker, had had employed her bouncy personality to personally ensure that the seats would be strong enough for the Green Army and that claims made by manufacturers about being unbreakable were true. Seats from five different companies were given consideration after two people at a time – including Liz – had jumped up and down on them and tried to bend them out of shape by hand. Liz, who was the auntie of Pilgrims' midfielder Martin Barlow, said the tests were meant to represent 'normal' wear and tear.

BARRS OPEN

AFTER Argyle acquired their long-term hold on Home Park in 2001, Barrs Construction were contracted to build three-quarters of a new stadium. Barrs built their offices on an all-weather pitch adjoining the Argyle car park. The pitch, with floodlights and changing facilities, had been financed by the Sports Council 12 years earlier. Working from the Barn Park end around to the Devonport end, Barrs first demolished the terracing and stands. A webcam was installed so that supporters could watch the rapid redevelopment of the ground, and each day, significant progress could be seen.

NEW YEAR, NEW ERA

THE 2001/02 season began with a reduced capacity at Home Park as work to rebuild three-quarters of the ground continued. However, the Pilgrims were in the Third Division, so the reduction to 7,500 was deemed unlikely to be a problem. Just four months after the contractors had arrived on site, the Devonport and Barn Park ends were opened for a Boxing Day 2-2 draw against Torquay, in front of a crowd of 13,677. A month later, the Lyndhurst Stand opened to complete the rebuilding of all but one side of the ground.

VILLAGE LIFE

FOLLOWING the reconstruction of the ground in 2002, the Argyle behind-the-scenes staff moved from their offices near the front entrance to the portable buildings that had been vacated by Barrs, nicknamed 'Argyle Village' by insiders. Over the seasons, the Village became a small conurbation with the addition of the Argyle Superstore and a hospitality marquee.

HOME AT LAST

ON December 19th, 2006, Argyle completed the purchase of the freehold of Home Park from Plymouth City Council in a £2.7m deal which saw the club become sole owner of the ground. Pilgrims' chairman Paul Stapleton said: "This is an important day in the history of Plymouth Argyle. For the first time since there has been an Argyle team playing at Home Park, we can truly say that it is now our ground." The price was largely thought to be a bargain. I mean, what can you buy for £2.7m these days?

WIZARD WINDRUM

ARGYLE played in the Southern League between 1903 and 1920, and their entry to the division was the result of a well thought-out strategy. If it had been the beginning of the subsequent century, someone with red braces and Dennis Taylor glasses would have called it a three-year plan, run it up the flagpole and saw who saluted. Clarence Spooner needed someone with inside knowledge to form a professional league club, and he turned to Lieutenant Frederick Hugh Windrum of the Royal Artillery, under whose guidance the very successful Royal Artillery (Portsmouth) football team had gained entry into the Southern League. With military precision, Windrum guided the Argyle Football Club through the organisational changes necessary if they were to be voted into the Southern League. On January 8th, 1903, the Plymouth Argyle Football Company Limited was formed, with Windrum as chairman, and he generated such publicity for Argyle that the entire football industry became excited about the prospect of expanding into new territory. For his part, Windrum was so certain of the outcome that Frank Brettell was appointed manager by Spooner a confident two months before the election, and, on Saturday, May 30th, 1903, Argyle easily obtained a majority vote to gain entry into the Southern League First Division. Argyle were Southern League champions in 1912/13, and were runners-up on two occasions, before joining the Football League Third Division (South) in 1920.

ARGYLE'S FIRST TEN SOUTHERN LEAGUE GAMES

Northampton Town (H) .... W 2-0
Brentford (A) .... L 0-1
West Ham United (H) .... W 2-0
Tottenham Hotspur (A) .... W 2-0
Luton Town (H) .... D 0-0
New Brompton (A) .... D 0-0
Kettering Town (H) .... W 5-1
Southampton (A) .... W 5-3
Millwall (A) .... L 0-1
Fulham (H) .... W 1-0

FIRST CLASS

ARGYLE beat West Ham United 1-0 away in the Western League in their first game as a professional club on September 1st 1903. Their first Southern League game was on September 5th, when they beat Northampton Town 2-0 in front of a crowd of 4,438. Stand tickets cost six pence (that's 6d, not 6p) and gate receipts were £124. The team was: Robinson, Fitchett, Clark, Leech, Goodall, Digweed, Dalrymple, Anderson, Peddie, Picken and Jack. Luckily for club historians and trivia buffs, the first goalscorer in each match (okay, the only goalscorer in the West Ham match) was the same, Jack Peddie.

A SET OF JACKS

IT is a lovely and little-known fact that the man who scored the first two goals in Argyle's history had the middle name 'Hope'. Scot John Hope Peddie, inevitably known throughout his career as, variously, Jack Peddie or Jock Peddie, was born in Hutchinsontown, Glasgow, on March 3rd 1876. A 5ft 11ins, 12st 6lb striker, he began his playing career with Benburb FC in Scotland before moving to Third Lanark in June 1895. After a successful trial at Newcastle two years later, he moved across the border and turned professional. He played in the North East for five years before moving to Manchester United in 1902. A year later, he moved on again, this time to Home Park and his date with destiny. Peddie stayed at Home Park for a single year. He made 46 appearances in the Southern League, Western League and FA Cup, scoring 21 goals. For good measure, he completed a hat-trick of firsts when he scored in professional Argyle's first ever FA Cup game – a 7-0 home win over Whiteheads. After his lone season in Devon, Peddie moved back to Manchester United, where, during the next three years, he became captain. He ended his career back in his native Scotland, with, first, Hearts and, then back in amateur football, before emigrating to America, ending up in Detroit, where he died in 1928, aged 52.

BEST WESTERN

ARGYLE'S first honour as a professional outfit came the season after they joined the Southern League, when they were crowned champions of the other league in which they played, the Western League, in 1904/05.

NOT EXACTLY SHAKESPEARE

THERE were some great names in the Argyle squad in their first, Southern League season, 1903/04. The likes of Winterhalder, Dalrymple, Fitchett and Leech to name just a few. At that time, Albert Webb, a poet, and a prolific writer of verse, produced works which were, in their own special way, classical. He wrote the following piece of work for a dinner held to celebrate Argyle becoming a professional football club. It was printed on the menu cards distributed on the night, and many of the 1903 players, and manager Frank Brettell, are included in the poem.

A: Is for Argyle, the team of the West
B: Is for Banks, a player of zest
C: Stands for Chadburn, who works with a will,
D: For Dalrymple, of grit and of skill.
E: Our Endeavour, club's motto and aim.
F: Is for Fitchett, we all know his fame.
G: For the Goals our players will get.
H: For the Harvest they'll reap for you yet.
I: The Intention, to bring Argyle luck.
J: Is for Jack, and his colleague, young Buck.
K: Stands for Kindness, this so far we've had.
L: Is for Leech, a fine, stalwart lad.
M: For the Manager, Frank's one of the best.
N: Nil Desperandum, its meaning you've guessed.
O: For Opinion, 'tis the public, our friends.
P: Stands for Peddie, and the strength which he lends.
Q: Is for Question, may our future be bright.
R: For Robinson, our goalie of might.
S: The Spooners, their worth we well know.
T: For the Trainer, good fellow, I trow.
U: Is for Union, this we must have to win.
V: For the Vanguard, the ball to put in.
W: Winterhalder, whom spectators all cheer.
X: The X'penses we all hope to clear.
Y: Stands for You, help to further our aim.
Z: For the Zenith Argyle hope to gain.

ROARING 40

UP to and including Paul Sturrock's reappointment in November 2007, forty men have been in charge of Argyle's fortunes – singly, jointly, permanently or temporarily – since the Pilgrims entered the Southern League in 1903, although only Bob Jack has shouldered the burden for more than ten years. Jack was manager twice, between 1905-06 and 1910 and 1938. Vic Buckingham is arguably the shortest 'serving' manager. Former Spurs defender Buckingham had agreed to take charge of the Pilgrims after Jack Rowley resigned in March 1960 but he changed his mind two weeks after being appointed and joined Sheffield Wednesday instead. He never saw his team in a competitive match.

THE ARGYLE MANAGERS

1903-1905 ..... Frank Brettell	1983-1984... John Hore
1905-1906 ..... Bob Jack	1984 .... Martin Harvey*
1906-1907 ..... William Fullerton	1984-1988... Dave Smith
1910-1938 ..... Bob Jack	1988-1990... Ken Brown
1938-1947 ..... Jack Tresadern	1990 .... John Gregory*
1948-1955 ..... Jimmy Rae	1990-1992... David Kemp
1955-1960 ..... Jack Rowley	1992 .... G Nisbet/A Gillett*
1960 .... Vic Buckingham	1992-1995... Peter Shilton
1960 .... N Dougall/G Taylor	1995 .... Steve McCall
1961 .... Neil Dougall	1995 .... Russell Osman*
1961-1963 ..... Ellis Stuttard	1995-1997... Neil Warnock
1963-1964 ..... Andy Beattie*	1997-1998... Mick Jones
1964-1965 ..... Malcolm Allison	1998-2000... Kevin Hodges
1965-1968 ..... Derek Ufton	2000 .... Kevin Summerfield*
1968-1970 ..... Billy Bingham	2000-2004... Paul Sturrock
1970-1972 ..... Ellis Stuttard	2004 .... Kevin Summerfield*
1972-1977 ..... Tony Waiters	2004-2005... Bobby Williamson
1977-1978 ..... Mike Kelly	2005 .... Jocky Scott*
1978 .... Lennie Lawrence*	2005-2006... Tony Pulis
1978-1979 ..... Malcolm Allison	2006-2007... Ian Holloway
1979-1981 ..... Bobby Saxton	2007 .... T Breacker/D Bulpin*
1981-1983 ..... Bobby Moncur	2007-2009... Paul Sturrock

denotes temporary/caretaker manager

BOB'S YOUR UNCLE

ARGYLE'S manager for a majority of their Southern League years was Bob Jack, whose appointment was the making of the club. Bob, a Scottish winger, was among the tranche of players who joined Argyle in 1903 when they turned professional and entered the Southern League, and was appointed player-manager in 1905. After a respectable fifth-place finish, he dropped down a division with Southend. After two Southern League Second Division titles, he returned to Home Park as manager and club secretary. This time, he lasted just a little bit longer. After winning the Southern League title in 1912/1913, he was at the helm as Argyle became a Football League club in 1920; when they won their first ever title in 1930; and still there in 1938, when he retired.

SECONDS OUT

FIVE of Argyle's forty managers have served two terms in the Home Park hot-seat. Bob Jack's second tenure between 1910 and 1938 was longer than the other four's combined service, although Ellis Stuttard was as loyal a Pilgrim as they come. A Lancastrian, he played 40 times for the club in various defensive positions and returned as manager in November 1961, taking the team to a fifth-place Second Division finish – a position the Pilgrims have not equalled since. He could not repeat the feat and was sacked in 1963. Worse was to follow when he was appointed Exeter City manager, but he was soon back at Home Park as chief scout for Billy Bingham. When Bingham went in 1970, Stuttard was reappointed manager but could not lift Argyle out of the Third Division and was relegated back to chief scout in 1972. He remained at Home Park for another ten years in a number of roles before he was made redundant. He died two years later, aged only 64.

TWO-TERMER MANAGERS

Bob Jack 1905-1906, 1910-1938
Ellis Stuttard 1961-1963, 1970-1972
Malcolm Allison 1964-1965, 1978-1979
Kevin Summerfield 2000*, 2004*
Paul Sturrock 2000-2004, 2007-09
* denotes temporary/caretaker manager

BOB JACK: 29 YEARS AS MANAGER AND HE NEVER REVERSED THE CHARGES ONCE

STORM BEFORE THE CALM

IF Robert Jack's settling managerial presence dominated the Pilgrims' early years as a Football League club, the polar opposite occurred in the early 1960s. Having won promotion to the Second Division in 1958/59, Jack Rowley found the temperature of the Argyle hot-seat too torrid the following season and walked in March. For the first time in Argyle's history, two men were put jointly in charge of the first team: former players Neil Dougall and George Taylor. They were helped by Jess Lowe, who was brought in as an administrator. The arrangement did not work and, after Vic Buckingham accepted, then turned down, the offer to manage the Pilgrims (alone), Taylor was demoted to chief trainer, leaving Dougall in sole charge. Remarkably, he kept Argyle up but lasted only a few months before another reshuffle, with Ellis Stuttard moving from assistant-trainer to manager, Dougall being demoted to coach/trainer, and Taylor remaining as chief trainer. Argyle's fortunes improved immediately.

PLAYER MANAGERS

FIFTEEN of Argyle's forty managers have also been Pilgrims players before or during their management, or, in the case of John Gregory and Steve McCall, after it. Indeed, Gregory did not make his Pilgrims debut until after he had been replaced as manager. Brought in to play by Ken Brown in February 1990 after a spell as Portsmouth manager, Gregory had not pulled on his boots before he was given temporary charge of the Pilgrims' first-team after Brown's dismissal. Gregory did not feel that Argyle's plight at the wrong end of the Barclays Second Division merited his skills and declined to pick himself for the two games he was caretaker-manager. However, Brown's permanent successor, David Kemp, immediately turned to the former England midfielder and gave him his playing debut – two years after his previous playing appearance – in a 3-0 home win over Sunderland on March 3rd 1990. Ian Holloway famously came out of retirement to play for the Pilgrims' reserves during his time in charge – for a game at Liskeard – but he does not count as a player and manager for the Pilgrims. These do: Bob Jack, Jimmy Rae, Jack Rowley, Neil Dougall/George Taylor, Ellis Stuttard, Bobby Saxton, John Hore, John Gregory*, David Kemp, Gordon Nisbet*, Peter Shilton, Steve McCall, Kevin Hodges, Kevin Summerfield*.

* denotes temporary/caretaker manager

PUFFED AS A BADGER

IAN Holloway came out of playing retirement in 2006 to help the Pilgrims out of a manpower shortage caused by them being committed to two games on the same night – at Swindon, in the Pontins Combination League, and at Cornish side Liskeard, in the South Western League. "I have heard he is a bit fat, slow and ugly but we needed some experience," said Holloway, of his new signing, i.e. himself. Lining up in central midfield, seven years after he had previously played seriously, alongside nine kids and one other player with Football League experience, he did manage the full 90 minutes, but to no avail, as Argyle lost 3-0.

EIGHT HAUL

EIGHT of Argyle's forty managers have won one promotion with the Pilgrims. Five of them were – or, indeed, still are – Scots. Bobby Williamson would probably baulk at being included on the list below, but the fact remains that he was manager when the Pilgrims won the last ever Nationwide Second Division, even if the 2003-04 title arrived in his first game in charge, a 2-0 home victory over QPR. The groundwork had been laid by Paul Sturrock, who left for Premiership Southampton with 12 games of the season remaining, and his former and soon-to-be-again assistant Kevin Summerfield, who held the reins for nine matches until Williamson's appointment. Although Williamson was manager for the title-winning game, his role was nominal – Summerfield selected the team, famously leaving out captain Paul Wotton.

UP THE GREENS

Bob Jack	Third Division (South)	1929/30
Jimmy Rae	Third Division (South)	1951/52
Jack Rowley	Third Division	1958/59
Tony Waiters	Third Division	1974/75
Dave Smith	Third Division	1985/86
Neil Warnock	Third Division	1995/96
Paul Sturrock	Third Division	2001/02
Bobby Williamson	Second Division	2003/04

ST PAUL

PAUL Sturrock was named as the Second Division manager of the season by the League Managers' Association in 2003/04. Despite leaving the Pilgrims for Southampton with 12 matches of the 2003/04 season remaining, Sturrock's input was enough for him to garner a majority of the votes from the Second Division managers.

SUMMERS TIME

IF Bobby Williamson had been appointed one game later, Kevin Summerfield would have joined Bob Jack as being a two-term manager who played for the club and who won a promotion. What is more, he was also promoted as a player, from the Third Division under Dave Smith in 1986. Despite being caretaker-manager twice, his lifetime influence at Home Park, both as a player and Paul Sturrock's right-hand man, should not be overlooked. Summerfield signed for Argyle in 1984 after doing the rounds at most of the Black Country clubs and soon established himself as one of the best attacking midfielders to have pulled on the Green. A regular for three seasons, he hit the slippery slope when, after personally dominating the early stages of an FA Cup replay against Everton at Goodison Park, his leg was broken in a tackle by Graeme Sharp. Jettisoned by Argyle after 162 games and 34 goals, he became a keystone of the Shrewsbury side in the early 1990s and returned to Home Park to knock his old side out of the League Cup with two goals in a first-round tie. It was at Shrewsbury that he began coaching, and he returned to Home Park as youth coach in 1997. Kevin Hodges' dismissal as manager in October 2000 opened the way for his first stint as Argyle's caretaker, and he was retained by Hodges' successor Paul Sturrock as the two men struck up an empathy that has seen them work together at Southampton, Sheffield Wednesday, Swindon and twice at Slymouth – sorry, Plymouth. His second spell in temporary charge was a difficult nine games between Sturrock's departure for Southampton and Bobby Williamson's appointment, but he kept the good ship Pilgrim on course for one of three promotions in which he has been a prime mover.

MOST MANAGER OF THE MONTH AWARDS

PAUL Sturrock (5): September 2001, October 2001, February 2002, October 2003, December 2003.

A WILF I LIKE

WILF Carter is the only man to have scored five goals for Argyle in a single Football League match, achieving the feat on December 27th 1960, when the Pilgrims beat Charlton Athletic 6-4 in a Second Division game at Home Park. The previous day, the Addicks had duffed Argyle at the Valley by exactly the same score. Carter, who is second in the list of the club's all-time top goalscorers, liked getting his goals in groupings. He has scored more hat-tricks than any other Pilgrim, with eight in total – seven league, one FA Cup – between 1957 and 1962. Someone at Charlton must have upset Wilf big time as, not only was his five-goal haul against the Addicks, he also scored two hat-tricks against the same team, with all the three games coming in a three-year period. Only on one other occasion has a Pilgrim scored five goals in a proper match, when H. Swann went nap (as football writers used to say) in a 5-0 home win against Millwall in the Western League in 1906. That was so long ago that poor old history-making Mr. Swann's first name is unknown. I like to think it was Hieronymus. Sam McCrory and Neil Langman both scored six goals in a game, but they came in friendly matches when Argyle toured the USA in 1954. Langman's double hat-trick came in an 8-4 win against the St. Louis All Stars in St. Louis. McCrory's was in a 16-2 victory over Colorado All Stars in Denver.

WILF'S MAGNIFICENT SEVEN (+ 1 FA CUP)

7th December 1957 .... FA Cup v Dorchester (H)................... W 5-2
14th December 1957 ...... Third Division (S) v Coventry (H) ..... W 4-0
15th Feb 1958 .... Third Division (S) v QPR (H)........... W 3-1
18th October 1958.......... Third Division (S) v Mansfield (A) .... W 4-1
3rd October 1959 .... Second Division v Charlton (H) .... W 6-4
27th December 1960 ...... Second Division v Charlton (H) ...... *W 6-4
6th March 1961 .... Second Division v Leeds (H).............. W 3-1
27th October 1962.......... Second Division v Charlton (H) .... W 6-1

THE FIRST TEN TO SCORE FOR ARGYLE

Peddie, Picken, Robinson, Winterhalder, Leech,
Jack, Anderson, Wheaton, Banks, Buck.

FOURMIDABLE

TEN Pilgrims have scored four goals in a single game since Argyle entered the Football League, with two of the ten achieving the feat twice. The last player to score four goals in a game for a second time was Mike Bickle, the former Co-op milkman, who delivered a quartet against Torquay in a Third Division 1969 Boxing Day encounter at Home Park. A little more than three years earlier, and up a division, Bickle had creamed four goals in a 7-1 battering of Cardiff, also at Home Park. However, Maurice Tadman achieved the feat inside just a couple of months of a purple patch that began with a couple at Torquay in a Third Division (South) game before he spanked Aldershot with four goals in a 5-1 win on October 14th, 1950. He netted his second four-goal haul away to Brighton – becoming the only Pilgrim to hit a quartet of goals away from Home Park – on November 18th, having, in the intervening three games, scored another (you guessed) four goals.

FOUR-TIMERS

Date	Player	Opponent	Result
3rd Feb 1923	Frank Richardson	FAC v Bradford PA (H)	W 4-1
16th Jan 1926	Jack Cock	D3(S) v Norwich (H)	W 6-3
27th Aug 1927	Freddie Forbes	D3(S) v Merthyr Tydfil (H)	W 5-0
21st Dec 1929	Tommy Grozier	D3(S) v Crystal Palace (H)	W 6-1
19th Apr 1930	Jack Vidler	D3(S) v Norwich (H)	W 4-1
17th Oct 1931	Jack Leslie	D2 v Nottingham Forest (H)	W 5-1
4th Jan 1936	Sammy Black	D2 v Port Vale (H)	W 4-1
14th Oct 1950	Maurice Tadman	D3(S) v Aldershot (H)	W 5-1
18th Nov 1950	Maurice Tadman	D3(S) v Brighton (A)	W 6-1
15th Oct 1966	Mike Bickle	D2 v Cardiff (H)	W 7-1
26th Dec 1969	Mike Bickle	D3 v Torquay (H)	W 6-0
5th Nov 1988	Tommy Tynan	D2 v Blackburn (H)	W 4-3

LEASE BE HAVING YOU

IN July 2001, Argyle were granted a new 125-year lease on Home Park, the City Council giving the club full legal possession of the site with proprietary ownership rights.

SOUTHERN BOYS

ARGYLE were Southern League champions in 1912/13, having previously twice been runners-up, in 1907/08 and 1911/12.

HAT-TRICK HEROES

BETWEEN December 15th 1903, when Wattie Anderson popped three goals in to help the Pilgrims to a 4-1 Southern League victory over Wellingborough, and February 18th 2006, when Vincent Péricard netted all three goals in a 3-1 home Championship victory over Coventry, a total of 62 players scored 101 hat-tricks for the Pilgrims. Both Wattie and Vincent probably peaked on those afternoons. Indeed, Anderson died of pneumonia after insisting on playing through illness for the Pilgrims in a 1-0 defeat against Fulham at Craven Cottage less than three months after his history-making triple. Péricard also suffered following his moment of glory. He was jailed for four months after being found guilty of perverting the course of justice while at Home Park during his loan from Portsmouth. Clocked at 103mph in his Mercedes CLK 500 on the approach to Plymouth, he told police that his step-father had been driving at the time. That'll be the step-father that police quickly discovered had not visited Britain for more than three years. Whoops a daisy. Following his early release from prison, Péricard experienced problems with his electronic tag, and was rearrested to serve more time inside.

THREE IS THE MAGIC NUMBER

FRANK Richardson, who was signed by the Pilgrims from non-league Barking Town, made his Argyle debut on the opening day of the 1921-22 season, August 27th, and scored all three goals as Argyle beat Bristol Rovers 3-1 in a Third Division (South) game. It was the first Football League hat-trick for Argyle and Richardson was the first Pilgrim to score a treble on his debut. He made it a hat-trick of hat-tricks by January 28th, having netted three-goal hauls against Swansea and Brentford. He must have had a thing about hat-tricks, because he scored one of the first FA Cup hat-tricks for Argyle against Bradford Park Avenue in 1923.

OOH LA LA (LA)

ARGYLE'S 100th hat-trick was the first to be scored by an overseas player. Appropriately, David Friio's moment of history came in the Pilgrims' centenary season of 2003-04, which they crowned by winning the Nationwide Second Division. Argyle were already well on their way to a 7-0 Home Park thrashing of Chesterfield when French midfielder Friio netted in the 16th minute to make the score 4-0, Lee Hodges, Tony Capaldi and Nathan Lowndes having preceded him in the scoring stakes. Lowndes and Friio doubled their individual tallies before half-time, but it was not until the dying minutes against a slightly more resilient Chesterfield side in the second half when Friio headed home substitute Ian Stonebridge's corner. Or did he? "I was so up for my hat-trick, I didn't head the ball properly, so I scored with my mouth," he said. The result was also Argyle's biggest home win since 1936.

FALL GUYS

THE PILGRIMS have scored seven goals at Home Park on 13 occasions. Remarkably, eight of those magnificent sevens have come in either September or October.

SEVEN GOALS AT HOME PARK

31st Oct 1903	FA Cup	Argyle 7 Whiteheads 0
1st May 1924	Third Division(S)	Argyle 7 Southend United 1
6th Sep 1924	Third Division(S)	Argyle 7 Brentford 1
10th Apr 1925	Third Division(S)	Argyle 7 Bristol City 2
26th Sep 1925	Third Division(S)	Argyle 7 Aberdare Athletic 2
25th Oct 1925	Third Division(S)	Argyle 7 Bournemouth 2
12th Feb 1927	Third Division(S)	Argyle 7 Crystal Palace 1
12th Oct 1935	Second Division	Argyle 7 Barnsley 1
5th Sep 1936	Second Division	Argyle 7 Doncaster Rovers 0
28th Oct 1950	Third Division(S)	Argyle 7 Colchester United 1
22nd Aug 1962	Second Division	Argyle 7 Preston North End 1
15th Oct 1966	Second Division	Argyle 7 Cardiff City 1
3rd January 2004	Second Division	Argyle 7 Chesterfield 0

DAVID FRIIO: LET HIS MOUTH DO THE TALKING

EASY AS TOFFEE

ANOTHER player to score a hat-trick on his Argyle debut was wing-half Norman Mackay, who netted three times in a 4-0 Third Division (South) victory over Coventry City at Home Park on January 28th 1928. The Scot was resurrecting a career that seemed to have stalled irrevocably after failing to make the grade with Aston Villa, for whom he played just twice. He ended up playing non-league football for Welsh works team Lovell's Athletic, where he was employed as a toffee salesman. An Argyle scout spotted him (playing football, not selling toffee) and offered him a way back into the professional game. It is fair to say that he took the opportunity. He remained at Home Park for a further six seasons, making 241 appearances, none of which could match his crash-bang-wallop debut. In fact, he scored only another 11 goals in the subsequent 240 matches.

CUP TREBLES

HARRY Wilcox scored Argyle's first hat-trick in the FA Cup when the Pilgrims beat Isthmian League New Crusaders 6-3 in an away qualifying round on January 13th 1906. Mike Bickle was the last Pilgrim to claim a hat-trick in an FA Cup tie, when Corby Town were dispatched from Home Park on January 22nd 1966, having lost a third-round tie 6-0. The only Argyle League Cup hat-trickster is Frank Lord, who scored all the Greens' goals in a fourth-round 3-1 Home Park replay victory against Stoke City on November 11th 1964. Lord was a goal machine who would have been worth millions had he played 40 years later. In his career, he boasted a near 1 in 2 goal-to-game ratio. Since Lord's day no Argyle player has scored more than two career hat-tricks while at Home Park and just five can claim a triple double: Derek Rickard, Tommy Tynan, Dwight Marshall, Steve Castle and Paul McGregor.

KING CASTLE

MIDFIELDER Steve Castle scored Argyle's quickest ever hat-trick when he notched a treble in a 3-2 Endsleigh Second Division game at Stockport on December 17th 1993. The Argyle captain led by example, scoring in the 50th, 55th and 56th minutes at Edgeley Park, an experience he later rated higher than playing in the last ever game at the old Wembley Stadium.

THREE OUT OF THREE

BETWEEN them, Jack Picken and Jasper McLuckie scored three hat-tricks in the space of 11 days in the 1904/05 season. Picken scored all three goals in a 3-2 home Southern League victory over New Brompton on October 8th, and followed that with a triple in a 5-0 Western League drubbing of Tottenham Hotspur on October 19th. In between, on October 12th, McLuckie popped three in against Queens Park Rangers, also in the Western League, to give Argyle a 3-0 win.

THE NEARLY TEAM

ARGYLE entered the Football League in 1920, and, after one season in a unified Third Division, were placed in Third Division (South), the winning of which earned promotion. You got, as Billy Bremner was to later immortalise as the title of his autobiography, nowt for coming second. Crushingly, Argyle proceeded to occupy the runners-up spot on each of the next six seasons. They missed out a by a minute goal average to Southampton in 1921/22; to Bristol City by six points in 1922/23; to Portsmouth by four points in 1923/24; to Swansea Town by a point in 1924/25; to Reading, also by a point, in 1925/26; and to Bristol City – again – by two points in 1926/27. They tailed off in 1927/28, ending up in third, and the following year were not in sight of the finishing-post. However, they came storming back in 1929/30, finally winning promotion by seven clear points from Brentford.

THIRD DIVISION (SOUTH)

Year	First	Second	Third
1921/22	Southampton	Argyle	Portsmouth
1922/23	Bristol City	Argyle	Swansea Town
1923/24	Portsmouth	Argyle	Millwall
1924/25	Swansea Town	Argyle	Bristol City
1925/26	Reading	Argyle	Millwall
1926/27	Bristol City	Argyle	Millwall
1927/28	Millwall	Northampton	Argyle
1928/29	Charlton Athletic	Crystal Palace	Northampton
1929/30	Argyle	Brentford	QPR

HEEPS' HISTORIC GOAL

ARGYLE'S Football League debut goal was, perhaps fittingly, scored by the only Pilgrim making his Argyle debut. The first goal came, at the second attempt, from Scottish youngster Jimmy Heeps. It was scored after half an hour of the 1920/21 Third Division season opener against Norwich City at Home Park, when, after failing to convince the referee that his first effort had crossed the line before being saved, Heeps headed the resultant corner home. Norwich spoiled the occasion by equalising midway through the second half and the game ended 1-1. Heeps, who had arrived at Home Park from Banknock Juniors, played 15 more times that season before returning north of the border to Airdrieonians. He did not score again for the Pilgrims.

SAINTS ALIVE

THE heartbreaker to end all heartbreakers from the Nearly Team of the 1920s came at the end of the 1921/22, season, the first time they were pipped to top spot – and how Argyle were the first club in the Third Division to win 61 points in a season, achieving the mark when they beat QPR 4-0 on April 29th 1922 to go two points ahead of Southampton. The final matches of the season took place the following week and Argyle lost 2-0 away to QPR; Southampton won and were promoted on a better goal average... of just 0.6130952 of a goal. Fred Titmuss was playing for Southampton that season – he later joined Argyle and was captain when the Pilgrims eventually won promotion.

BIG APPETITE

AFTER finally winning promotion in 1930, by beating Newport away on Easter Monday, April 21st, Argyle were able to enjoy the final few games of the campaign. Everyone was in a celebratory mood for the last match of the season on May 3rd when Watford arrived in town, and captain Freddie Titmuss was the beneficiary of a very special gift, a massive 'oggie' – or Cornish pasty, to the rest of the world. *The Western Independent* described the scene. "Two men, the focus of 25,000 pairs of eyes, walked steadily across Home Park. They bore with them, reverently, on a species of stretcher, a large, nicely browned, and bulging pasty, which, with all solemnity, they presented to Titmuss, the Plymouth Argyle captain."

REPEATING ON ME

MORE than 70 years after Argyle captain Freddie Titmuss was presented with a giant pasty before a league game against Watford to mark the Pilgrims winning promotion to the Third Division (I know, I know, the captain of any other club would have got a rose-bowl or something), the classic episode from Argyle history was re-enacted before Argyle played Watford in the FA Cup quarter-final on March 11th 2007. Pilgrims captain Paul Wotton was presented with the three-foot pasty, lovingly baked and generously donated by the shirt sponsors Ginsters, before the 6pm kick-off. Wottsy, resisted the temptation for a pre-match scoff, the good-luck charm was paraded around Home Park on a stretcher, and then placed behind the goal for a few minutes for its charm to take effect. Watford players got over their astonishment to score the only goal of the game and prevent Argyle from reaching the FA Cup last four for only the second time in their history. The first time they did, they had lost to Watford.

EAR WE GO

GEORGE Reilly was the scorer of the goal that dashed Argyle's Wembley dreams when the Third Division Pilgrims lost 1-0 to Watford in the 1984 FA Cup semi-final at Villa Park. Nearly 20 years later, Reilly was working as a bricklayer on a building site in Northamptonshire when he was the victim of an unprovoked attack by another worker who bit off part of his right ear before whispering one word in Reilly's other, unchewed, ear – "Plymouth".

100 UP

DURING the two Third Division (South) seasons of 1921/22 and 1922/23, Argyle were unbeaten at home, with their Home Park goal analysis reading Goals For 90; Goals Against 10.

SUMMING UP

BETWEEN 1921-1927, the six seasons when Argyle were Third Division (South) runners-up, they played 252 matches, won 143 and drew 55.

SHALL I? SHAN'T I?

ATTENDANCES at Home Park in the early days reflected not only the team's performance, but also the fact that there was a big rugby following in the three towns at that time. If the rugby club was playing well, Home Park attendances would drop. In Argyle's first season as a professional club, they had 5,000 to see them qualify for the FA Cup, but 20,103 turned up to see them play reigning First Division champions Sheffield Wednesday in the first round.

HE WHO ABERDARES...

BETWEEN September 1925 and January 1927, the Pilgrims played Aberdare Athletic four times in the Third Division (South), winning three times and losing once, scoring 16 goals and conceding 13. They began with a 7-2 home win in the 1925/26 season, which the Welsh side reversed at the Athletic Ground later by winning 6-1. A year after the nine-goal feast at Home Park, the Pilgrims could manage only a 2-0 win, but made up for that low-key affair by winning the away return by the odd goal in 11 – and I'll wager that phrase will never be used in any future report of an Argyle game.

ARGYLE v ABERDARE ATHLETIC 1925-27

26 September 1925 (H) .... W 7-2
6 Feb 1926 (A).. L 1-6
4 September 1926 (H) .... W 2-0
22 January 1927(A) .... W 6-5

WAR CHAMPIONS

AFTER the Football League was suspended three games into the 1939/40 season because of the Second World War, Argyle competed in the South West Regional League, alongside Bristol City, Bristol Rovers, Cardiff City, Newport County, Swansea Town, Swindon Town and Torquay United. Each side played each other four times. Argyle started with a 4-0 shelling of Torquay and a 6-0 blitz of Bristol City on their way to winning the 28-game competition. Their biggest win was a 10-3 defeat of Bristol City in front of fewer than 900 spectators, during which Jackie Smith scored four goals.

JACK'S 72

AFTER the Second World War, Home Park was described as "a picture of desolation with the grandstand reduced to a heap of rubble at the bottom of a huge crater; the grass had grown long, and debris covered parts of that formerly well-kept playing pitch". Pilgrims' manager Jack Tresadern had been a member of the serving forces – he was at least 45-years-old when he was called up – and, while Home Park was being renovated, he virtually single-handedly built a new team. When hostilities ended, there was still a large contingent of forces personnel in and around Plymouth, and Tresadern recruited many of these to fill gaps in his team. In the first transitional season after the war, when Argyle played in the Football League (South), he used 72 players. Sometimes it was a case of whomever he could get, and, on away matches, the coach had to make detours to pick up players on the way to the ground. In that season, 17 players were from the armed services and 27 were guests from other league teams.

ARGYLE GUEST PLAYERS 1945-46

B. Brown	Queens Park Rangers	3
L. Latham	Aston Villa	1
G. Cole	Chester	1
J. Logie	Arsenal	1
E. Carless	Cardiff	11
J. Prescott	Hull	5
J. Court	Cardiff	4
T. Swinscoe	Chesterfield	1
H. Cumner	Arsenal	2
F. Scrine	Swansea	2
J. Dryden	Charlton	1
F. Sargent	Tottenham	1
R. Ferrier	Oldham	1
A. Squires	Preston	2
J. Gardiner	Wolves	8
D. Smale	Chelsea	3
K. Griffiths	Cardiff	2
R. Sinclair	Chesterfield	1

R. Haddington	Bradford	3
E. Taylor	Newcastle	2
F. Haycock	Aston Villa	1
J. Tivendale	Watford	9
J. Hunter	Preston	1
A. Tomlinson	Blackburn	7
J. Kirkham	Bournemouth	1
W. Whittaker	Charlton	1
A. Kerr	Aston Villa	3

SPANNING THE DIVIDE

WHEN competitive football restarted after the Second World War, the Football League decided that the fixtures for the abandoned 1939/40 season should be repeated for the 1946/47 campaign. On August 26, 1939, Argyle had lost 3-1 at home to West Ham United: on 31 August 1946, they reversed that scoreline. The only player to play in both of those matches was Len Jones. Despite the impressive start, Argyle finished 19th in the league table, conceding 96 goals.

TRAVELLING BLUES

WHEN the fixture computer throws up a fixture that sends Argyle to Hull on a Tuesday in December, spare a thought for the team that played in the 1945/46 Football League (South) season. These were the Christmas fixtures:

December 21st.......away to Birmingham City
December 25th....... away to Manchester City
December 26th......home to Manchester City

The team travelled, by train, to Birmingham on December 20th, for their match the following day against the Blues, which they lost 6-1. They stayed overnight in Birmingham then journeyed to Manchester and played City on Christmas Day, losing another seven-goal game 4-3. Both the Argyle and City teams then caught the 5.30pm train to London, where they linked up with the overnight train to Plymouth so that they could play again on Boxing Day, after arriving at 6am that morning. Argyle completed a festive hat-trick by losing 3-2.

ONE GAME, ONE GOAL

THOMAS Swinscoe's one appearance for Argyle during the transitional 1945/46 Football League (South) season put him in the record books. The Chesterfield centre-forward's goal in a 4-1 defeat by Chelsea on Easter Monday, April 22nd 1946, means that he is one of only two Pilgrims to score a goal in his only Argyle appearance. The other was Peter Middleton, of whom great things were expected when he signed for the Pilgrims in the autumn of 1972 from Bradford City. His debut, in a Third Division game against Shrewsbury Town at Home Park, appeared to endorse that expectation as he opened the scoring in a 3-0 victory with a superb solo goal and thereafter generally terrorised the Shrews' defence. Sadly, such promise was never fulfilled as Peter was knocked down by a car as he went to a public telephone box to call Home Park to speak about travel arrangements for the next game. He badly damaged his back, never played again and, in April 1977, having been blighted by depression caused by his premature retirement, he took his own life. He was just 28.

WAR HERO

THE word 'hero' is overused in football but entirely appropriate in the case of John Demmelweek. The right-winger joined Argyle from the Royal Navy as an amateur in 1926 but later turned professional and stayed with the Pilgrims until 1935, making 34 appearances, scoring two goals, before moving to Southend. When the Second World War broke out, he rejoined the Royal Navy and took part in Operation Chariot, a successful British attack on the heavily-defended docks at St. Naziare in occupied France on the night of March 28th 1942. An obsolete destroyer, HMS *Campbeltown*, was used to ram the lock-gate and then blown up to destroy the dock to make it difficult for German ships like the *Tirpitz* to get repairs done. Five servicemen were awarded the Victoria Cross, but 168 men were killed in the raid and 214 – including Demmelweek – were taken prisoner of war, and saw no further action. Winston Churchill was aware of the *Tirpitz's* capabilities and was "desperate" to see it destroyed. Hubert Powell, a Plymouth man who was in the RAF Reconnaissance Unit, spotted the *Tirpitz* and photographed her in the North Sea, near Tromso. RAF Bomber Command used the photographs to identify and sink the ship in November 1944.

BRAVE PILGRIM

ANOTHER former Argyle war hero was Evelyn Henry Lintott, who played twice for the Pilgrims in the 1906/07 season. Lintott had attended St. Luke's College and went on to play left-half for England. Later, he was a lieutenant in the West Yorkshire Regiment's 15th Battalion during the First World War. He was on the Somme at the end of June 1916, when artillery had been pounding the German front line for a week, and went over the top of the trenches in daylight. More than 19,000 men lost their lives on that first day – including Lintott – the world's bloodiest day in history. The battle raged on until November, by which time more than one million people had lost their lives – enough people to fill Home Park every Saturday for a year.

BACK FROM THE DEAD

John Gilbert 'Jack' Cock was the first Cornishman to play for England, a war hero, and an actor with a great singing voice. Born in Hayle, he started his professional career with Huddersfield Town shortly before the First World War broke out. He served in the army, rising to the rank of sergeant-major and earning the Distinguished Conduct Medal and Military Medal for gallantry. He was reported as 'missing, presumed dead' but was later found, very much alive, and played for England in the Victory International in 1919. He made his proper England debut against Ireland in 1919, opened the scoring after 30 seconds – the third-fastest England goal – and won a second and final cap against Scotland in 1920, again scoring. After the war, Cock was sold to Chelsea for a record £2,500 and scored twice on his debut. He was top scorer at Stamford Bridge in 1920/21 and 1921/22 before transferring to Everton in February 1923. Cock remained on Merseyside for two years, before coming home to Argyle in March 1925. He scored 74 goals in just 92 games, including 32 in 39 Third Division (South) games in 1926/27 – a club record that still stood more than 80 years later. After Argyle, he moved to Millwall and scored 92 goals in 135 appearances, helping the club win the Third Division (South) title in 1927/28, at the expense of Argyle. Thanks, Jack. Good-looking and possessed of a sweet tenor voice, Cock appeared on the music-hall stage numerous times and starred in several films, including *The Winning Goal* (1920) and *The Great Game* (1930).

CHOO'D OUT

CHRISTMAS travel has never been easy for the Pilgrims. When they kicked off before losing a Second Division game 9-1 at Everton on December 27th 1930, they had been on Merseyside less than nine hours following an overnight train journey that had arrived in Liverpool at after 6am. Ten hours earlier, they had left Plymouth on the evening of a home match against Cardiff, which they had won 5-1.

STEAMING IN

ARGYLE fans have always been used to travelling long distances, so the Green Army have often amused themselves by trying different ways of going to away matches. Charabanc parties and special train excursions were organised by Devonport Dockyard employees in the days when the Yard thrived, particularly for FA Cup ties. Nothing they did could top the trip to Swansea just after the Second World War, though. On the Easter weekend of April 5th 1947, the Greens were playing Swansea Town in a Second Division match and some Argyle fans who lived in North Devon took an Ilfracombe Paddle Steamer Company ride across the Bristol Channel to watch the match. They were a part of a 22,000 crowd who saw the Pilgrims sunk 3-1. The Argyle scorer was the South African left-wing Billy Strauss.

TEST CHARACTER

THE only Pilgrim to play cricket for England was Welshman Allan Watkins, who represented Argyle between 1946 and 1948 and England between 1948 and 1952. In fact, Watkins played more Tests for England (15) than games for Argyle (five). A left-handed batsman, medium-to-fast left-arm bowler, and a brilliant close fielder, he was the first Glamorgan cricketer to score a century in Tests. He netted just one goal for the Pilgrims, in a 3-2 Second Division home defeat by Southampton in 1947 on, appropriately enough, St. David's Day.

TIGHT AS DRAKE'S DRUM

BETWEEN 1920-1930, Argyle conceded fewer goals than any other club in the Football League.

GETTING THE UMP

THE only Pilgrim to become a first-class cricket umpire was Barrie Meyer. He scored eight times in ten matches during the 1958/59 title-winning season. Meyer also played football for Bristol Rovers and City, as well as Newport County and Hereford United. He could not settle in Plymouth, which explains his brief but explosive spell at Home Park. A wicketkeeper, he played for Gloucestershire in more than 400 first-class cricket matches between 1957 and 1971 and later became a cricket umpire. He umpired 26 Tests in England between 1978 and 1993, including the famous 1981 Ashes Test at Headingley. He also umpired 23 one day internationals (1977 to 1993), including World Cup Finals at Lord's in 1979 and 1983.

A LOT OF FLANNEL

ONE of the most famous cricketing Pilgrims was George Dews, who scored 81 goals in 271 games for the Greens between 1947 and 1955. He missed the beginning of each of those eight seasons, however, as he was on duty with Worcestershire. He made his Worcestershire debut before his Pilgrims one, and suffered a king pair. He was also out for a duck in his third innings, and it was not until 1950 that he really came good, breaking the 1,000-run barrier for the first time, a feat he would repeat in all but one year for the rest of his first-class career. His most successful year was 1959, when he scored 1,752 runs at 41.71 in all first-class cricket and was second in the Worcestershire batting averages. He was never picked for England, but did appear for MCC in 1954. Gentleman George's first game for Argyle was in November 1947 after joining from Middlesbrough and his most successful season the 1951/52 promotion-winning year, in which he scored 25 goals.

GRECIAN BURN

ARGYLE'S record win in their Devon derbies against Exeter City came in January 1957, when goals from Eric Davis (2), Neil Langman, Jack Rowley, and an own goal gave the Pilgrims a 5-0 Third Division (South) victory at Home Park. Their biggest defeat was a 4-0 Third Division (South) beating on Christmas Day, 1925. Exeter fans will no doubt take delight from the fact that, ultimately, the loss cost Argyle promotion to the Second Division as they finished the campaign just a point behind Reading.

DERBY DEBUTS

ARGYLE played their first Devon derby against Exeter City on November 11th 1908, losing 2-1 at their neighbours. Centre-half Charlie Clark scored the goal. The first derby against Devon's other senior club, Torquay United, was on November 5th 1927, also away, which the Pilgrims won 2-1, with goals from Freddy Forbes and Sammy Black. Argyle have since played Exeter another 89 times and Torquay another 49 times up to the end of the 2008/09 season. As you would expect from the Westcountry's senior team, defeats by their fellow Devonians have been relatively few and far between with the pair managing just 35 wins from 150 games (Exeter 24, Torquay 11). Argyle have scored 126 goals against Exeter and 95 against Torquay, conceding 89 and 54 respectively.

RAZOR-SHARP BICKS

THE Pilgrims' biggest margin of victory over their nearest neighbours, Torquay United, was a 6-0 Third Division Home Park smashing on Boxing Day 1969, when Mike Bickle scored four goals. Norman Piper got the other two. Apart from a 5-2 defeat at Plainmoor during the Second World War, the Pilgrims have conceded more than two goals in a game to the Gulls only three times. They won the last of these, 4-3, in an Endsleigh Third Division game – when Adrian Littlejohn claimed a hat-trick – at Home Park in 1995, and the first, by the same score, in a Third Division (South) match at Plainmoor in 1929. However, sandwiched in between was a 3-2 away Third Division (South) defeat on December 8th 1951.

LAPPING IT UP

FORWARD Mike Bickle was playing semi-professionally in the South Western Football League, with St Austell, when, at 22, he signed for Argyle in December 1965, giving up his job as a milkman. Cream rises, as they say, and pretty soon Bicks was delivering in the Second Division. He scored nine goals in 17 games in his first half-season and went on to be the club's top goalscorer for the following four seasons, scoring 71 goals in 179 league matches. He then joined former Pilgrims team-mate Andy Nelson, who had taken over as manager of Gillingham, in Kent after weeks of press speculation. He retired in 1973 after damaging his shoulder.

THERE'S ONLY ONE...

OR is there? A quick Google of some famous Argyle names reveals that: Mike Bickle is actually the director of the International House of Prayer in Kansas City, and Adrian Littlejohn is the minister of music at First Baptist Church in Gastonia; Billy Rafferty owns Doggy Dooz Pet Styling; Michael Evans is a full-time professional fly fishing instructor, tackle designer, writer and filmmaker; Kevin Summerfield is a writer/producer/director, founder of Scorpio Pictures, and CEO of Online InterMedia LLC, an interactive news network media agency; Leigh Cooper is a graphic designer in Wanaka, New Zealand; David Kemp is President of the Victorian Branch of the Liberal Party; Steve McCall is Senior Lecturer in Education, Visual Impairment, at the University of Birmingham; Martin Barlow is the leading international expert in diffusion on fractals and other disordered media based at the University of British Columbia; Sean McCarthy is Chief Financial Officer and Secretary of Diedrich Coffee, Incorporated; Jack Chisholm was lead guitarist with the Chevelle Five; Norman Piper is an amateur photographer with a DPAGB and an AFIAP to his name; Paul Wotton is Senior University Clinician in Veterinary Cardiology at Glasgow Veterinary School; Kevin Hodges is a former Major League Baseball and Nippon Professional Baseball pitcher; and Nicky Jennings was Scottish ladies' showjumping champion.

HULL HELL

PETER Shilton survived more than a quarter of a century without being sent off, during games for Leicester City, Stoke City, Nottingham Forest, Southampton, Derby County and England. However, the introduction of a new law governing back passes to the goalkeeper in 1990 put paid to that. Player-manager Shilts simply could not cope with the rule and ended up seeing red for the first time in August 1992, after committing a professional foul in a game at Hull City. Defender Nicky Marker went in goal and saved the resultant penalty, but the ten men ended up losing 2-0.

GREENS ON SCREEN

ARGYLE'S first appearance on *Match of the Day* was in a Third Division game away to Luton Town on January 17th 1970. The Pilgrims won 2-0, with goals from Derek Rickard and Mike Bickle.

MIKE BICKLE: THE OTHER ONE

COME AND SEE…

MORE than half of the top 20 largest crowds to have watched Argyle at Home Park did so in a January FA Cup tie. Indeed, nine of the top 12 home attendances were for cup ties, including the topmost gate of all time, 44,526 against Huddersfield Town on January 13th 1934. Nine of the top 20 occurred in the 1930s, including the highest ever league crowd (and second-best overall) when 43,596 crammed into Home Park on October 10th 1936 for a 2-2 Second Division draw with Aston Villa, and one of only two games in the top 20 that Argyle won – the highest crowd to see a Home Park win was the 36,344 who paid to see a 5-1 Second Division victory over Bury on Boxing Day 1931. The post Second World War boom in attendances also made its mark on the Pilgrims, with six of the top 20 highest crowds occurring in Second Division and FA Cup games between January 1948 and December 1952.

TOP 12 HOME PARK ATTENDANCES

Jan 13th 1934 .... 44,526 v Huddersfield Town (FA3) .... D 1-1
Oct 10th 1936 .... 43,596 v Aston Villa (D2) .... D 2-2
Jan 26th 1935 .... 41,403 v Bolton Wanderers (FA4) .... L 1-4
Jan 27th 1962 .... 40,040 v Tottenham Hotspur (FA4) .... L 1-5
Jan 6th 1951 .... 40,000 v Wolverhampton W (FA3) .... L 1-2
Jan 7th 1950 .... 40,000 v Wolverhampton W (FA3) .... D 1-1
Jan 10th 1949 .... 40,000 v Notts County (FA3) .... L 0-1
Jan 18th 1929 .... 38,159 v Bradford Park Avenue (FA4) .... L 0-1
Jan 4th 1958 .... 38,129 v Newcastle United (FA3) .... L 1-6
Dec 26th 1936 .... 37,242 v Fulham (D2) .... L 0-3
Dec 26th 1931 .... 36,344 v Bury (D2) .... W 5-1
Jan 10th 1959 .... 36,247 v Cardiff City (FA3) .... L 0-3

ARGYLE MEN WHO ALSO PLAYED CRICKET

Allan Watkins, Glamorgan and England; George Dews, Worcestershire; Barrie Meyer, Gloucestershire; John Mitten, Leicestershire; Ernie Carless, Glamorgan; Geoff Crudgington, Staffordshire, Minor Counties; Jack Chisholm, Middlesex, Minor Counties; Billy Strauss, Minor Counties; Derek Ufton, Kent.

LOW EIGHTIES

IF the 1930s and post Second World War eras were the best of times for the Pilgrims, there is no doubt that the early 1980s were the worst: 14 of Home Park's lowest 20 crowds came in the two years between September 12th 1981 and October 15th 1983, when the Pilgrims were an average Third Division team. The gates of those 14 games combined would not top the single best attended game at Home Park. The single worst attended home game in any of the three main competitions came on August 24th 1999, when Nationwide Third Division Argyle entertained Walsall in the second leg of a Worthington Cup first-round tie. The fact that the Pilgrims were already 4-1 down in a competition in which they had an appalling record probably had something to do with it. In fact, you might ask why even 1,834 bothered to turn up. Those 1,834 were probably posing themselves the same question after Argyle lost the second leg by the same margin as the first. At least they were consistent.

LOWEST 12 HOME PARK ATTENDANCES

Aug 24th 1999 ....1,834 v Walsall (LC) ....L 1-4
Oct 31st 1903 ....1,870 v Whiteheads (FAQ1) ....W 7-0
Nov 14th 1903 ....2,500 v Freemantle (FAQ2) ....W 5-1
Sept 15th 1981 ....2,348 v Chester (LC) ....W 1-0
Oct 19th 1982 ....2,525 v AFC Bournemouth (D3) ....W 2-0
Oct 24th 1981 ....2,646 v Chester (D3) ....W 5-1
Sep 29th 1981 ....2,745 v Reading (D3) ....D 1-1
Aug 23rd 1994 ....2,801 v Walsall (LC) ....W 2-1
Apr 30th 1983 ....2,912 v Preston North End (D3) ....D 1-1
Oct 16th 1982 ....2,921 v Lincoln City (D3) ....L 0-2
Oct 15th 1983 ....2,990 v Oxford United (D3) ....W 2-1
Oct 21st 1997 ....3,003 v Burnley (N2) ....D 2-2

FOUR STAR HAULS

HONOURABLE mentions in the four-goals-a-game category should be given to Freddie Buck, Fred Burch and Bert Bowler, who were three prolific Argyle players to score four goals in a game before the Pilgrims entered the Football League. Jackie Smith also managed a quartet, his in a 10-3 home win against Bristol City in the wartime South West Regional League.

TRIPPING HIGHS

NEARLY half of Argyle's top 20 highest away attendances have come in the cups, the FA Cup or League Cup. It is hardly surprising given these have been really the only time they play big clubs in big grounds with big followings. The highest crowd that the Pilgrims have ever played in front of was at Highbury, where they lost 4-2 to Arsenal in the fourth round of the FA Cup on January 23rd 1932 – that was some 6,000 more than saw a third-round repeat of the tie at the Emirates on January 3rd 2009, when Arsenal won 3-1. The biggest crowd in front of which Argyle have not lost is the 59,871 at Stamford Bridge who witnessed a 0-0 draw between the Pilgrims and Chelsea on February 24th 1921. The biggest crowd in front of which Argyle have won was at Hillsborough, where, on January 14th 1950, they won a Second Division game against Sheffield Wednesday 4-2 in front of 39,316, with goals from Frank Squires (2), Billy Strauss and George Dews.

ARGYLE'S TOP 12 HIGHEST AWAY ATTENDANCES

1 Jan 23rd 1932............65,386 v Arsenal (FA4)..................................L 2-4
2 Feb 24th 1921..........59,871 v Chelsea (FA3R)............................D 0-0
3 Jan 3rd 2009.............59,424 v Arsenal (FA3)...................................L 1-3
4 Jan 25th 1936............53,704 v Chelsea (FA4)..................................L 1-4
5 Aug 23rd 1947.........52,642 v Newcastle United (D2) ....L 1-6
6 Dec 7th 1946 ....45,000 v Newcastle United (D2) ....L 2-3
7 Feb 27th 1954..........44,496 v Everton (D2).................................L 4-8
8 Apr 14th 1933 ....44,483 v Tottenham Hotspur (D2) ....D 0-0
9 Apr 14th 1984 ....43,858 v Watford at Villa Park (FA SF)........L 0-1
10 Jan 11th 1950...........43,835 v Wolverhampton W (FA3R)...........L 0-3
11 Jan 30th 1937...........42,430 v Tottenham Hotspur (FA4) ....L 0-1
12 Feb 13th 1937..........42,000 v Aston Villa (D2).............................L 4-5

BYO REF

WHEN Argyle toured South America in the summer of 1924, they took a referee with them, Freddie Reeve, who was the chairman of the Western Division Referees' Association.

THEY CAME IN THEIR DOZENS

THREE of Argyle's four lowest away attendances have occurred in May, when there has been nothing to play for. Indeed, the lowest league or cup gate and the fourth-lowest came in two miserable consecutive weeks at the end of the 1984/85 Canon Third Division season, in which Argyle finished 15th. On May 4th 1985, just 1,435 paid to see them draw 1-1 against Cambridge United at the Abbey Stadium, while 89 fewer attended the Den on May 11th to watch the Pilgrims end the campaign with a 2-0 defeat, the 1,346 being the lowest gate in front of which the Pilgrims have ever played.

ARGYLE'S LOWEST 12 AWAY ATTENDANCES

1. May 11th 1985 .... 1,346 v Millwall (C3) .... L 0-2
2. Oct 22nd 1973 .... 1,432 v Rochdale (D3) .... W 3-1
3. May 1st 1993 .... 1,432 v Wigan Athletic (B2) .... W 2-0
4. May 4th 1985 .... 1,435 v Cambridge United (C3) .... D 1-1
5. Jan 14th 1928 .... 1,500 v Merthyr Town (D3S) .... W 4-1
6. Dec 23rd 2000 .... 1,670 v Halifax Town (N3) .... L 0-2
7. Sep 8th 1981 .... 1,690 v Chester (LC) .... D 1-1
8. Mar 23rd 1974 .... 1,715 v Halifax Town (D3) .... L 0-1
9. May 1st 1974 .... 1,722 v Cambridge United (D3) .... L 1-3
10. Oct 20th 1998 .... 1,791 v Brighton & Hove Albion (N3) .... W 3-1
11. Apr 5th 1993 .... 1,822 v Hartlepool United (B2) .... L 0-1
12. Mar 4th 1995 .... 1,823 v Chester City (E2) .... L 0-1

FLIGHT OF FANCY

GIVEN their geographical location, it is no surprise that Argyle were the first English club to consider flying to away games, back in 1932 – but the League Management Committee declined permission. The request came from club president Albert Casanova Ballard, known as 'Archie' and later dubbed the Pied Piper of Plymouth. He was quite a character: he had no known relatives, may have been born under another name, was less than five feet tall, and was legendarily generous. When he arrived in Plymouth, he started a boys' club, later known as the Ballard Institute. In 1937, he celebrated King George VI's coronation by presenting the boys with a National Provincial Bank book each, with an entry for £5 – double the average weekly wage in those days.

GOOD EVANS

ANOTHER famous goal celebration was that of Argyle legend Michael Evans. Micky was playing in his final match at Home Park on April 30th 2006, the end-of-season Coca-Cola Championship clash with Ipswich Town, when he headed the winner in the 59th minute in front of the home support in the Devonport end. Immediately, he was pounced upon by all ten team-mates, including goalkeeper Romain Larrieu, disappearing under the mound of bodies.

DRAWING OUT THE AGONY

IN 1963/1964, Argyle escaped relegation to the Third Division only by a superior goal average than Grimsby Town, a relatively large margin of difference of 0.04 of a goal. The Pilgrims kept their fans on tenterhooks by drawing their last four matches of the campaign, 1-1 at Norwich City and Leeds United, and 1-1 at home to Cardiff City, and, on a tense final day, 0-0 against Rotherham United at Home Park.

COP THAT

ARGYLE'S Second Division game against Oxford United in October 1975 was not an arresting match, although the Pilgrims won 2-1, thanks to two Paul Mariner goals. It did contain a moment of merriment for the crowd and embarrassment for one local police constable when Oxford defender Roger Hynd kicked the ball into touch to prevent Mariner from adding to his tally. The ball flew straight at the policeman and knocked his helmet off.

GREEN ENVIRONMENT

ARGYLE were the very first visiting team to play at Kenilworth Road, home of Luton Town, in a Southern League match on September 4th 1905. The game was dominated by one colour. Argyle wore their traditional green strip, the referee was a Mr. Green, as was the Luton Town club secretary and, as it was the first match at the ground, a commemorative kick-off was performed by a family member of the local brewers… Greene King. The game ended 0-0.

MICHAEL EVANS: "IN 15 YEARS' TIME, I'M GOING TO GET MOBBED"

OTHER ATTENDANCES OF NOTE INVOLVING ARGYLE

May 16th 1963 .... 100,000 .. Warsaw Legia (A, Tour) .... L 1-2
May 18th 1963 .... 50,000 .... KSC Lech (A, Tour) .... L 0-1
May 21st 1963 ..... 60,000 .... BWKS Lechia (A, Tour) .... W 3-0
May 23rd 1963 .... 40,000 .... SC Turbine (A, Tour) .... L 2-3
Mar 14th 1973 ..... 37,639 .... Santos (H, Friendly) .... W 3-2
Jul 21st 2006 .... 1,500 ...... Real Madrid (Austria, Friendly) .... L 0-1
Dec 9th 1961 .... 12,907 .... Reserves v Spurs Reserves (H) .... L 1-4
Aug 11th 1946 ..... 8,000+ .. Probables v Possibles (H, friendly) ..... W/L 7-2
Jan 20th 1962 .... 25,648 .... Reserves v Mansfield Reserves (H) .... W 4-1

SOME EXPLANATIONS ON THE ABOVE

THE 1963 post-season tour behind the Iron Curtain was run in tandem with the 16th International Cycle Race for Peace, and the packed stadia had as much to do with Polish and East German enthusiasm for the bikes as it did with the Pilgrims. The 1961 match against Tottenham's stiffs was the first game back in England played by Spurs' Jimmy Greaves after his brief Italian sojourn, while Tottenham also played their part in boosting the gate for the 1960 game against Mansfield's second string, at which tickets for the upcoming FA Cup match between the Pilgrims and Spurs went on sale.

SIMPLY THE VEST

SEAN McCarthy scored his 200th career goal whilst playing for Argyle, on February 19th 2000 in a Third Division game against York City at Home Park. Team-mates Chris Hargreaves and Paul McGregor shared in his celebration, with the trio taking off their shirts to reveal T-shirts bearing the numbers '2', '0' and '0'. The undergarments were presumably beginning to whiff a bit since McCarthy had scored his 199th goal against Torquay United eight games earlier.

LONG TIME COMING

THE Pilgrims had been a professional club for 46 years before they suffered their first relegation, from the Second Division to Third Division (South) in 1950.

SEMI SADNESS

THE Pilgrims have never won a cup – unless you count the Devon Professional Bowl – but have twice reached the last four of the League Cup. The first time was in 1964/65, the year after they were nearly relegated to the Third Division. They beat Sheffield United, at home; Bury, away; Stoke City, at home after a replay; and Northampton Town, at home, before losing over two legs to a top-flight Leicester City side that included England goalkeeper Gordon Banks. They lost the first leg at Filbert Street 3-2, where Johnny Williams and Mike Trebilcock scored, and the Home Park return 1-0. Nine seasons later, the Third Division Pilgrims missed out on a Wembley final when they went out to eventual winners Manchester City, again over two legs. The first leg was at Home Park – which was packed to the gunwales despite being played on a Wednesday afternoon because of a power crisis – and ended 1-1, with Steve Davey scoring, but City won the Maine Road resumption 2-0. On the way to the last two, Argyle had accounted for Torquay United, away; Portsmouth, home; and top-flight trio Burnley, Queens Park Rangers and Birmingham City, all away.

VALE OF TEARS

PETER Shilton's Second Division team of 1993/94 was largely held to be one of the most attractive of Argyle's lower league sides, but, although they were the division's leading scorers, with 88 goals, they finished third in the table, three points behind runners-up Port Vale. Their opponents in the play-off semi-final were Burnley, who had finished 12 points behind the Pilgrims in the regular season. After a 0-0 draw at Turf Moor in the first leg, all appeared to be going with form, and that opinion was franked when Dwight Marshall gave Argyle a 1-0 lead back at Home Park in the second leg. Then it all went wrong as Burnley's John Francis helped himself to two goals to put Burnley on the way to a 3-1 win.

YOUNG COLTS

ARGYLE had a Colts side which played in the Western League for two seasons. They finished 16th in 1966/67, after winning 12 of their 40 matches, and improved to ninth the following season, when they were triumphant 18 times.

WEMBLEY WINNERS

TWO seasons after missing out on a Second Division play-off place, Argyle reached Wembley for the first and only time in their history when Neil Warnock's side beat Colchester United 3-2 over two legs to earn a promotion-or-bust Endsleigh Third Division encounter against Darlington at Wembley on Saturday, May 25th 1996. Midfielder Ronnie Maugé scored the only goal of the game, heading home Mark Patterson's cross in the 66th minute, to ensure his place alongside Warnock in Pilgrims' legends, yet Maugé would probably not have been playing had Gary Clayton not picked up an injury in the last-but-one match of the regular season. Incidentally, Argyle had beaten neither Darlington, nor Colchester United in the league that season, losing twice to their final opponents and losing away and drawing at Home Park with Colchester, who also beat the Pilgrims in the first leg of the play-off semi.

VIENNESE WHIRL

ARGYLE played First Vienna on Saturday, January 28th 1933 at Home Park in front of 16,000 spectators. The result was 1-1 with Eugene Melaniphey getting the Argyle equaliser five minutes from time. The pitch was frozen, which did not help the Austrians. After the match, the players of both teams dined with the Lord Mayor and Lady Mayoress at the Duke of Cornwall Hotel. Every Argyle player received a Vienna club buttonhole and Argyle manager Robert Jack presented silk handkerchiefs to the Vienna players.

RHYS LIGHTNING

ARGYLE goalkeeper Rhys Wilmot enjoyed some rather spectacular shooting on the Glorious Twelfth, August 12th 1989. Goalkeeper became goal-poacher against South Western league side Porthleven in a pre-season friendly at Gala Parc, scoring an 11-minute hat-trick.

WHERE THERE'S A WILL...

THE first own goal to be credited for Argyle came in a Western League match against Brentford on September 14th 1904, when Williams Davidson netted in a game that the Pilgrims won 6-1.

LEAGUE CUP WINLESS

BETWEEN October 1992 and August 2005, Argyle did not win a single League Cup tie, going out of the competition at the first hurdle in 11 straight seasons. The rot set in at the third-round stage of the 1992/93 competition when, after having beaten West Bromwich Albion and Luton, and with a glamour tie against Arsenal awaiting, Peter Shilton's Barclays Second Division side went out to Football League newcomers Scarborough. The following season, the Pilgrims beat Birmingham 2-0 at Home Park, after losing the first leg at St. Andrews 3-0. The next season they beat Walsall 2-1 at home – having already lost the opening leg 4-0 – and that was the last time they tasted any sort of victory for 11 long years. Along the way, some ignominious results were achieved: back-to-back 4-1 thrashings by Walsall, and a 5-3 home defeat by Oxford United for a 7-3 aggregate tanning. The sorry sequence ended on August 23rd 2005, when goals from Paul Wotton and Scott Taylor saw Bobby Williamson's Championship side squeeze past Peterborough 2-1 at Home Park.

LEAGUE CUP LOSERS

1993/94	R1 (1st leg)	Birmingham City (A)	0-3
	R1 (2nd leg)	Birmingham City (H)	2-0
1994/95	R1 (1st leg)	Walsall (A)	0-4
	R1 (2nd leg)	Walsall (H)	2-1
1995/96	R1 (1st leg)	Birmingham City (A)	0-1
	R1 (2nd leg)	Birmingham City (H)	1-2
1996/97	R1 (1st leg)	Brentford (A)	0-1
	R1 (2nd leg)	Brentford (H)	0-0
1997/98	R1 (1st leg)	Oxford United (A)	0-2
	R1 (2nd leg)	Oxford United (H)	3-5
1998/99	R1 (1st leg)	Portsmouth (H)	1-3
	R1 (2nd leg)	Portsmouth (A)	2-3
1999/00	R1 (1st leg)	Walsall (A)	1-4
	R1 (2nd leg)	Walsall (H)	1-4
2001/02	R1	Watford (A)	0-1
2002/03	R1	Crystal Palace (A)	1-2
2003/04	R1	Colchester United (A)	1-2
2004/05	R1	Yeovil Town (A)	2-3

CRAWFORD'S CRACKER

STEVE Crawford scored one of the most bizarre goals of his career in his brief stay with Bobby Williamson's Argyle during the 2004/05 Championship season. It came in a 3-2 League Cup first-round defeat by Yeovil Town at Huish Park after Lee Johnson had given the home side the lead. Johnson had inadvertently scored while trying to return the ball to Argyle goalkeeper Luke McCormick following treatment for an injury to Pilgrims team-mate Graham Coughlan. McCormick had moved off his line and Johnson's kick sailed into the back of the net from almost 50 yards. Immediately, Glovers manager Gary Johnson – Lee's dad – instructed his players to stand back at the restart and allow Crawford to walk the ball into the net and level the scores. Johnson said: "After Lee scored, I turned to Bobby Williamson straight away and said, 'Don't worry Bob, you'll be getting the next goal.' He's a big guy and calming him down was my first job. Then I got word to my players to let Plymouth go straight down the other end and stick the ball in the back of the net."

STADIUM OF PINT

AFTER Argyle beat Sunderland 3-2 in a Championship game at the beginning of the 2006/07 season, manager Ian Holloway made a generous offer to the 700 fans who made the 805-mile round-trip from the Westcountry. "I hope I see one or two of those on the Barbican over the next couple of days and I might like to buy them a drink," he said. "So anyone who travelled up here, please send me a letter – I'd love to buy you a drink." He was still dipping his hand into his pocket months later as he bumped into people in Plymouth who insisted they were on Wearside that afternoon.

MANAGEMENT BY COMMITTEE

AFTER Willie Fullerton was dismissed as Argyle manager, following a 15th-placed finish in the 1906/07 Southern League, the club carried on without a figurehead for three seasons. The management committee steered the Pilgrims to runners-up position in their first season but that appeared to be beginners' luck as the following two campaigns saw the Greens resolutely mid-table. It was then that the management committee made a far more sensible decision, to appoint Bob Jack.

2-0 AND WE DID RATHER WELL

ARGYLE'S longest spell without conceding a league goal – 642 minutes – was achieved by the 2003/04 title-winning team. The run started with a dramatic 3-2 win at Swindon on December 13th 2003; the Pilgrims were pegged back to 2-2 by a last-minute goal, only to nick the game 3-2 through Marino Keith's injury-time winner. The next goal they conceded came eight matches later, in the 12th minute of a 2-1 defeat at Brighton & Hove Albion. Luke McCormick was the goalkeeper and the ever-present back four were: Paul Connolly, Hasney Aljofree, Graham Coughlan and Peter Gilbert.

Dec 13th 2003......... D2......... Swindon (A) .... W 3-2
Dec 20th 2003......... D2......... Notts County (H)........................ W 3-0
Dec 26th 2003......... D2......... Bournemouth (A)........................ W 2-0
Dec 28th 2003......... D2......... Brentford (H).............................. W 2-0
Jan 3rd 2004 .... D2......... Chesterfield (H)........................... W 7-0
Jan 10th 2004 .... D2......... Grimsby (A)................................. D 0-0
Jan 17th 2004 .... D2......... Rushden & Diamonds (H).......... W 3-0
Jan 21st 2004 .... D2......... Stockport (A)................................ W 2-0
Jan 31st 2004 .... D2......... Brighton (A) .... L 1-2

FOREIGN LEGION

BETWEEN 1946-2009, Argyle had 40 overseas players: Billy Strauss (South Africa), Alfred Williams (South Africa), Crawford Clellend (USA), Danis Salman (Cyprus), Dwight Marshall (Jamaica), Mark Quamina (Guyana), Erik Van Rossum (Holland), Douglas Hodgson (Australia), Andy Petterson (Australia), Ronnie Maugé (Trinidad), Bruce Grobbelaar (Zimbabwe), Giancarlo Corazzin (Canada), Earl Jean (St Lucia), Romain Larrieu (France), David Friio (France), Sacha Opinel (France), Jean-Philippe Javary (France), Jason Bent (Canada), Osvaldo Lopes (France), Eugene Kangulungu (France), Jani Viander (Finland), Mathias Kouo-Doumbe (France), Bjarni Gudjonsson (Iceland), Taribo West (Nigeria), Bojan Djordjic (Serbia), Ákos Buzsáky (Hungary), Lilian Nalis (France), Vincent Péricard (Cameroon), Marcel Seip (Holland), Barry Hayles (Jamaica), Péter Halmosi (Hungary), Krisztián Timár (Hungary), Rory Fallon (New Zealand), Nadjim Abdou (France), Larrys Mabiala (France), Yoann Folly (France), Gyorgy Sandor (Hungary), Nicholas Marin (France), Emile Mpenza (Belgium) and Rudi Douala (Cameroon).

AN A-Z OF NICKNAMES

Angel: Eugene Kangulungu, in recognition of the good work he has done in his country (Congo).

Bamber: Brian Hall because he had a degree – Bamber Gascoigne used to compere the *University Challenge* quiz on television.

Cardiff: John L Williams; he came from Cardiff Juniors and it distinguished him from another John Williams on the books at the same time.

Chopsy: Martin Barlow, because, as a youngster, he used to answer – or chop – back at senior players.

Chuck: David Norris, after the all-action Hollywood film star, although the player preferred his boyhood nickname, Nosher.

Cucu: Péter Halmosi, a family nickname that was also applied to his Hungarian international father, Zoltan.

Dan: Marino Keith, after the American football quarter-back, Dan Marino.

Elastic: Milija Aleksic, because it is easier to say than 'Aleksic'.

Flash: Gordon Astall, because he was quick and Flash Gordon was a popular fictional creation at the time. Rather greedily, he had two nicknames and was also known as Cannonball because of the ferocity of his shot.

Gentleman George: George Dews, because he was a… well, a gentleman.

Hector: Mickey Heathcote, after a cartoon character of the same name.

Jacko: Sometime reserve-team manager, physio, kit-man and general factotum Ian Pearce, lookalike of Hollywood film star Jack Nicholson.

Jigsaw: Kevin Nugent, because he went to pieces in the box.

Jumbo: Jack Chisholm, because he was of a large stature.

Luggy: Paul Sturrock, because of the size of his ears, or, in Scotland, 'lugs'.

Mad Dog: Brian McGlinchey, after an Irish republican of the same name.

Penalty: John Peddelty, because manager Tony Waiters, preceding Jack Charlton by 15 years, could not find his way around his real name.

Rambo: Gerry McElhinney, after the Sylvester Stallone film character John Rambo, a troubled Vietnam War veteran and former Green Beret. It is not known whether Rambo played football, but Gerry McElhinney was harder.

Shelly: Paul Connolly, because of his love of shell suits.

Sloop: Coach John Blackley, because of his name and second initial: "We sailed on the sloop John B., my granddaddy and me…"

Trigger: Michael Evans, after the character in *Only Fools and Horses*.

Zimmer: Steve McCall, because he was getting on in years when he signed for the Pilgrims.

TV STARS

IN May 1972, an Argyle side won regional independent television station Westward's Six-a-side Competition, held at the Mayflower Centre adjacent to Home Park. Argyle's winning sextet was goalkeeper Peta Balac, John Hore, Derek Rickard, Colin Sullivan, Steve Davey and Ronnie Brown.

JOHN OF ALL TRADES

JOHN William Sutcliffe – known as J. W. – made 229 appearances for Argyle as a goalkeeper between 1904 and 1912. The total was all the more remarkable because he had started out his career as a centre-forward with Bolton Wanderers. After converting in what Argyle fans might call a 'Reverse Nizzie' manoeuvre, he won five England caps, and never finished on a losing side. He also won England caps at rugby, was a talented cricketer, and an excellent athlete. After retiring, he took up billiards and ice skating, at which, no doubt, he was nothing less than excellent.

ARGYLE'S FIVE MOST RECENT CHIEF EXECUTIVES

Liz Baker
Roger Matthews
David Tall
John McNulty
Michael Dunford

OOH AAR

ARGYLE Against Racism was launched on August 21st 2003. Explaining the group's establishment, a spokesperson said: "AAR members come from all age-groups, from teenagers to pensioners, and all walks of life. The group includes both black and white men and women. We all got involved for different reasons: bad experiences at Argyle matches, religious or other ideals, or simple disgust at the way our beautiful game loses out when racism rears its ugly head. We are also a democratic group, where decisions are made by majority consent, so we cannot be hijacked by any outside organisation or set of ideas."

TESTIMONIAL OPPONENTS

Aberdeen (Billy Strauss) .... D 2-2
Torquay United (Ellis Stuttard I) .... W 7-2
WBA/Tottenham Hotspur XI (Jack Chisholm) ... W 3-2
Sunderland (Jack Rowley) .... W 3-0
Burnley (Neil Dougall) .... L 1-6
All Stars (George Robertson I) .... L 2-4
Leicester City (Dave Corbett) .... L 3-4
Arsenal (Bill Harper) .... D 1-1
Manchester City (Mike Bickle) .... L 2-3
Liverpool (John Hore) .... L 3-4
Manchester United (Peter Middleton) .... L 1-2
Hereford United (Steve Davey) .... W 3-0
All Stars (Jim Furnell) .... W 3-3
Nottingham Forest (Ellis Stuttard II) .... L 1-2
Aston Villa (Brian Johnson) .... L 0-3
Chelsea (Chris Harrison) .... L 0-1
Blackburn Rovers (George Robertson II) .... W 2-0
Nottingham Forest (John Uzzell) .... W 6-1
West Ham United (Kevin Hodges I) .... D 3-3
Coventry City (Leigh Cooper) .... L 1-2
Tottenham Hotspur (Geoff Crudgington) .... L 0-3
Arsenal (Graham Little) .... L 0-2
Aston Villa (Tommy Tynan) .... L 1-2
Luton Town (Kevin Hodges II) .... D 2-2
Sheffield Wednesday (Adrian Burrows) .... L 0-5
Fulham (Martin Barlow) .... L 0-2
Torquay United (Dave Smith) .... W 2-1
Anderlecht (Paul Wotton) .... D 2-2
All Stars v Luggy's XI (Michael Evans) .... W 4-2

SECS APPEAL

ARGYLE have had nine secretaries since joining the Football League: Robert Jack, who was also manager; Jack Tresadern, likewise; A. H. Cole; P. Skinnard; Jess Lowe; P. J. Galvin; D. Rowe; Graham Little, who was also general manager; and Carole Rowntree.

JIM FURNELL: IN ONE OF HIS MORE EBULLIENT MOODS

TOO MUCH LIPA

TWO months after Argyle Against Racism was set up, Port Vale midfielder Andreas Lipa apologised to Plymouth midfielder Jason Bent over a racist comment he aimed at the Pilgrims' player. He was also fined a week's wages which were donated to the anti-racism Kick it Out charity, as well as AAR. "Andreas has written to Jason expressing his profound regret for the comment he made during Saturday's match, said in the heat of the moment and regretted immediately afterwards," revealed the official Argyle website, www.pafc.co.uk. Ironically, the alleged incident happened during the Football League's Anti-Racism Week of Action.

WAY TO GO

ON August 2nd 2002, Pilgrims' Way, was officially opened by Argyle chairman Paul Stapleton. Not to be confused with the historic route supposed to have been taken by pilgrims from Winchester in Hampshire, England, to the shrine of Thomas Becket at Canterbury in Kent, this Pilgrims' Way forms part of the entrance walkway at the Devonport End of Home Park. Argyle fans were invited to purchase a brick for the walkway, engraved with their own personal message.

STATS NICE

PILGRIMS Way is made up of 2,012 bricks, of which 1,185 are engraved in black (56%) and 917 in gold (44%). In addition, 46 replica bricks were bought for supporters' homes and businesses. Of these, 31 had gold engraving, and 15 had black engraving. The most popular engraved message is: FOREVER GREEN on 115 bricks, followed by ARGYLE FOREVER on 110; GREEN ARMY on 69; SEMPER FIDELIS on 52; LOYAL FAN on 41; and HAPPY BIRTHDAY on 32. There are 59 bricks 'In Memory of...' or 'Remembering...' a loved one. In addition, 309 bricks contain a date; 90 contain the name David or Dave; 79 contain the name John; 50 contain the name Michael or Mike; 50 contain the name Paul; and 47 contain the name Peter or Pete. One brick was a proposal of marriage; and 976 bricks (46%) were bought by supporters within the City of Plymouth boundary.

NOT IN FRONT OF AUNTIE

CORNISHMAN Mike Trebilcock played for non-league Tavistock before joining Argyle in December 1962. He scored 29 goals in 81 games for the Pilgrims, leading to a £23,000 move to Everton on December 31st 1965, and a dramatic impact on the public consciousness. Injury meant that he spent most of the rest of the season on the sidelines, but, despite this lack of activity, Toffees' manager Harry Catterick selected him ahead of England international striker Fred Pickering for the 1966 FA Cup Final against Sheffield Wednesday. Wednesday took a 2-0 lead with goals from Jim McCalliog and David Ford, but within five minutes of Ford's goal, Trebilcock scored twice to level the scores. A goal from Derek Temple sealed the win for Everton. It was his appearance in the final that led to a change in the pronunciation of his name. Known to Westcountry folk as 'Treble-cock', the association with fowl was obviously too much for genteel Auntie Beeb, who insisted on the more demure 'Tre-Bill-co'.

TIME FOR CHANGE

MANY Argyle fans missed the kick-off in the first few games of the 1979/80 Third Division season after being caught out by a rise in admission prices. Pay-on-the-day prices had been raised from £1 to £1.30 and fans were not bringing the correct money with them, causing delays in change giving. On top of that, there were also problems with the turnstiles running out of change. To overcome the problem, Argyle set up a change-kiosk so that supporters could go to the turnstile with the correct money.

RUNNING THINGS

TONY Waiters was a go-ahead manager. In his five years at the Home Park helm between 1972-75, he wanted more done to encourage young players to come to Plymouth as, from his previous work with the England youth team, who he led to victory in the 1973 European Youth Championship, he appreciated the need for developing young players. He brought in a far-reaching scouting system and was responsible for piloting the development of Harper's Park as a training ground. In order to raise money for, and awareness of, the project, Waiters ran a marathon (and then some) from Penzance to Plymouth. He was sponsored to the tune of £4,000.

BY GEORGE

THERE would be a few contenders for the title 'Mr Argyle', not least of all those christened with the name, but George Robertson would certainly be among them. He joined the Pilgrims as a player just after the Second World War, from Gairdoch Juniors, and was still active at the club nearly 40 years later. After 14 years as a player, the defender finished just 18 appearances short of joining the exclusive 400 club – but still not a bad number for a player who had considered giving up the game after a few matches for the Pilgrims reserves, convinced he was not good enough to make the grade. After hanging up his boots, Robertson continued to serve Argyle as, among other things, groundsman and manager of the club's youth hostel. He was rewarded with a second testimonial against Blackburn Rovers in 1986.

WITH GOD ON OUR SIDE

THE Reverend E. Reid once played in a friendly for Argyle. Rev Reid, who was from a church in Exeter, played against Bristol City at Home Park in October, 1905. City won 3-1.

HARRY CANNED

BILL Harper was already 34 and a Scottish international and league championship-winning goalkeeper when he arrived at Home Park in December 1931. However, any thoughts that he was winding down proved erroneous. He made his first-team debut against Bury on Boxing Day 1931, having already played for the reserves on Christmas morning – a match in which he saved two penalties. As Peggy Prior pointed out in her article on Harper for the Pilgrim matchday programme: "Although brought in primarily as a reserve player, Harper kept Harry Cann off the pitch for most of the remainder of the 1931/1932 season and missed only five matches the following year. He was between the sticks for the FA Cup fourth-round match against Arsenal at Highbury in January 1932, and contributed to the famous 8-1 thrashing of Millwall at Home Park that same month." He turned to coaching, played his last match in April 1939, aged 42, and later worked for the club as a trainer, groundsman and kit manager and generally helped out. In October 1972, Arsenal visited Home Park for his testimonial, and his name lives on at the club's training ground: Harper's Park.

ANTIQUE BOOK

ONE of the oldest players to make his professional debut in any of the English divisions was Tony Book, when he played his first game for the Pilgrims on the opening day of the 1964/65 Second Division season, a 2-0 defeat at Coventry City. Defender Book had followed his former Bath City manager Malcolm Allison to Home Park at the age of 30 for a fee of £1,500. The Plymouth board, though, believed him to be 28 – Allison had advised Book to doctor his birth certificate as he thought they would not pay £1,500 for a 30-year-old. The former bricklayer missed just three games in the two years he spent at the club before climbing on Allison's bandwagon again and moving to Manchester City after 93 games and three goals. Under Book's captaincy, Manchester City won four trophies, making him the most decorated Manchester City captain of all time. He also had a five-year tenure as Manchester City manager from 1974-1979, and subsequently held various coaching roles at the club until 1996. He later renewed his Argyle connections by becoming a scout for the club in the 21st century. Aged 304, or something.

FROZEN CRABB

EXETER referee Ron Crabb brought Argyle's home Third Division match against Bradford City to an abrupt end on February 18th 1978. It was postponed in the 61st minute, with Bradford winning through a 25th-minute goal from David McNiven, because of adverse weather conditions. Crabb, a prison officer who was in his last season as a referee, had no doubts about starting the game, but conditions deteriorated, particularly in the second half – sleet turned to hail and was driving relentlessly down the pitch. One of Crabb's watches had frozen and conditions got to the stage where he could not see one of the goals (insert own joke here). He finally called matters to a halt when his head went numb and he had problems breathing. He was still shaking an hour after the game had been called off. Perhaps Argyle midfielder Micky Horswill had been keen to get out of the weather, too. In the 23rd minute of the match, he made a two-fisted attack on Bradford's David McNiven, and, even though Crabb had blown to stop the game, continued to chase angrily after McNiven. Horswill rightly received a red card – and was jeered off by his own supporters.

MOOR TROUBLE

ON March 18th 1961, Argyle switched their pitch for Ipswich's visit (and say that after four pints of Pilgrim Ale) from White Hart Lane to Plainmoor. You what? Let me explain. On February 11th that season, Argyle fans had been rather less than pleasant towards referee Dennis Howell – the future Minister for Sport, no less – showering him with orange peel, paper cups and a beer bottle. You wonder what might have been aimed in his direction if the Pilgrims had lost their Second Division game to Huddersfield, rather than won it. Anyway, the Football League Management Committee decided to punish Argyle by closing Home Park, which meant they had to find a venue for their home game against Ipswich Town. White Hart Lane, the home of Tottenham Hotspur, was chosen initially but the venue was later changed to Torquay United where the Pilgrims lost 2-1 in front of only 9,626 fans.

BOARD ROOM

BACK in 1928, manager Robert Jack wanted the goals to be more visible so he painted yellow boards and had them erected behind each goal.

SHOPPING AROUND

FANS wanting to purchase Argyle paraphernalia from anywhere other than at Home Park had to wait until February 2004 before the club had a presence in Plymouth City Centre. The club opened a retail outlet in Derry's department store, Royal Parade. By the start of the 2005-06 season, the club also had a presence throughout most of Cornwall: Launceston Sports, Launceston; Studs Sports, Bodmin and Newquay; Trophy Textiles, Redruth; and Whirlwind Sports, Camborne and Penzance. In July 2007, the Pilgrims opened a new superstore in Plymouth's Drake Circus shopping mall, called the Argyle Centre Spot. Also selling tickets. "For the first time fans will be able to buy a ticket for our matches without needing to come up to Home Park," said chief executive Michael Dunford, when the opening was announced.

FOLLOWING SIR FRANCIS

IN August 1946, Argyle lost 94-78… playing bowls against the Peverell Park Bowling Club.

PALACE OF VARIETIES

JACK Fitchett, who was one of the first professional players to represent Argyle, was later manager… of the city's Palace Theatre. Full-back Fitchett, who was born in April 1880 in Manchester, made 46 appearances for the Greens in the 1903/04 season, joining from Bolton Wanderers and subsequently leaving for Manchester United. He also played for Southampton, Manchester City, Fulham and Exeter City before returning to Plymouth to take over the running of the Palace Theatre. The Palace Theatre opened as a music hall in Union Street in 1898. It was damaged by fire only eight months after opening, but re-opened in 1899 as The New Palace Theatre of Varieties. In 1961, it was converted to a bingo hall and continued in this use and as a theatre until 1983, when it became 'The Academy' disco. In May 2006, it closed after a police drug-busting operation. It has also been managed by former Argyle assistant-secretary and long-time employee Peter Hall.

NIFTY 50

ARGYLE were unbeaten in league and cup matches at Home Park for 50 games between April 2nd 1921 and August 25th 1923. The streak, comprising 47 Third Division (South)/Third Division games and three FA cup ties, began with an unpromising 0-0 draw against Southampton, and ended with a 2-1 defeat from the Saints' neighbours Portsmouth on the opening day of the 1923/24 season, Jack Fowler scoring for the Pilgrims. After two more wins at Home Park, they lost there again, 3-1 to Swindon Town. Thirty-seven of the games in the 50-match unbeaten home run saw the Pilgrims keep clean sheets; Argyle failed to score in just five of the games; the Pilgrims won 39 games and drew 11; the only side to score more than once in a match against them was Brighton & Hove Albion, who drew 2-2 on March 10th 1923; from September 3rd 1921, when the Pilgrims beat Bristol Rovers 1-0 until December 31st, when Swansea scored in a 3-1 defeat, Home Park did not witness an opposition goal in ten consecutive matches; between September 17th and November 12th 1921, Frank Richardson scored seven goals in five games; from March 11th 1922 to January 13th 1923, the Pilgrims conceded two goals in 18 matches, scoring 40 in reply; in the last seven games of the streak, between March 17th and May 2nd 1923, Jack Fowler scored nine goals.

HOT THOMAS

ARGYLE striker Dave Thomas's New Year's resolution for 1947 must have been 'score more goals'. From New Year's Day to the end of March, he scored in every single Argyle Second Division game. His hot streak started with the consolation strike in a 4-1 defeat at Chesterfield. He then netted in a 4-1 win against Sheffield Wednesday at Home Park; in a 3-1 defeat against Fulham at Craven Cottage; and in a 3-1 home victory over Bury. Dave then netted two goals in a 4-3 victory at Luton Town's Kenilworth Road; another in a 4-0 home triumph against Leicester City; and singles in a 3-2 home loss to Southampton; a 3-2 Home Park win over Barnsley; and defeats by Burnley, 2-1 at Turf Moor, and by Spurs at Home Park, 4-3 – 11 goals in 10 games. His brother Bob scored in the games against Sheffield Wednesday and Luton. After that, Thomas, who had also scored six goals in the 11 games prior to his club record streak, did not score until the second game of the following season. And, for the pedants, there was one game between January 1st and March 29th that he did not find the net, an FA Cup third-round tie at Chesterfield on January 11th, which the Pilgrims lost 2-0.

January 1st	Chesterfield (A)	1-4
January 4th	Sheffield Wednesday (H)	4-1
January 18th	Fulham (A)	1-3
January 25th	Bury (H)	3-1
February 1st	Luton Town (A) (scored twice)	4-3
February 16th	Leicester City (H)	4-0
March 1st	Southampton (H)	2-3
March 15th	Barnsley (H)	3-2
March 22nd	Burnley (A)	1-2
March 29th	Tottenham Hotspur (H)	3-4

SEVEN-YEAR ITCH

ARGYLE'S fourth promotion, and the first when they did not win the title, came in 1975, when a goal from Paul Mariner beat Colchester United 1-0 at Home Park on April 15th, to end a seven-year spell in the Third Division by way of finishing runners-up. Manager Tony Waiters' men were: Jim Furnell, John Hore, Brian Johnson, Paul Mariner, Hughie McAuley, Mike Green, Phil Burrows, Bobby Saxton, Billy Rafferty, John Delve, Colin Randell.

NINE STRAIGHT WINS I 1930

TWICE in their history has an Argyle team achieved nine successive league victories. The first side to do this was Robert Jack's 1929/30 Third Division (South) title-winning side. Their run began at Home Park on March 22nd, when two Sammy Black goals saw them beat Bournemouth and Boscombe Athletic 2-1, and ended at Crystal Palace in the third-last game of the season, where they lost 3-0. The goals were shared around, with Jack Vidler scoring nine, including an impressive four-goal haul against Norwich City at Home Park and a hat-trick, also at home, against Queens Park Rangers. Sammy Black hit five; Jack Pullen and Frank Sloan four; Ray Bowden three; and Norman Mackay and Tommy Grozier scored one each.

March 22nd............. Bournemouth & Boscombe Ath (H) 2-1
Black 2
March 26th.............. Swindon Town (H) 5-0
Bowden 2, Pullen, Sloan, Vidler
March 29th.............. Walsall (A) 3-1
Grozier, Bowden, Black
April 2nd .... Brighton and Hove Albion (A) 1-0
Vidler
April 5th .... Queens Park Rangers (H) 4-0
Vidler 3, Pullen
April 12th .... Fulham (A) 3-1
Pullen 2, Sloan
April 18th .... Newport County (A) 3-1
Sloan 2, Mackay
April 19th .... Norwich City (H) 4-1
Vidler 4
April 21st .... Newport County (A) 2-0
Black 2

PAGE-TURNER

THE oldest Plymouth Argyle matchday programme known to be in existence is for the Southern League fixture against Reading on September 29th 1906. The Pilgrims won 4-0, with a hat-trick from Tom McKenzie.

NINE STRAIGHT WINS II 1986

THE second time Argyle put together a club record nine straight wins shows some similarities to the first in 1929/30. It came at the same time of the year, beginning only a fortnight earlier than the original; it started with a 2-1 win; and it was from a Third Division promotion-winning team. The run of wins for Dave Smith's Argyle team began on March 8th 1986 away at Bristol Rovers, where goals from Russell Coughlin and Kevin Godfrey turned off the Gas. It was Godfrey's only Pilgrims goal in his seven-game loan spell from Leyton Orient. As had been the case 57 years earlier, the goals were shared about: Russell Coughlin, Kevin Hodges and Tommy Tynan scored four goals each; John Clayton and Kevin Summerfield hit three apiece; and there were solitary strikes for Leigh Cooper, Steve Cooper, Kevin Godfrey, Clive Goodyear, John Matthews and Darran Rowbotham. Rotherham's future England international Nick Pickering netted an own goal. It should be noted that four of Coughlin's 22 goals from 152 appearances came in the streak. Incidentally, the gate for the Wolves game was 2,367.

Mar 8th..................Bristol Rovers (A)..................2-1
Coughlin, Godfrey
Mar 11th..................Wolves (A)..................3-0
Coughlin, Summerfield, Clayton
Mar 15th..................Walsall (H)..................2-0
L Cooper, Coughlin
Mar 18th..................Chesterfield (A)..................2-1
Summerfield, Goodyear
Mar 22nd..................Derby County (H)..................4-1
Clayton 2, Rowbotham, Hodges
Mar 28th..................Cardiff City (A)..................2-1
Hodges, Matthews
Apr 5th..................Bournemouth (A)..................3-1
S Cooper, Coughlin, Hodges
Apr 8th..................Rotherham United (H)..................4-0
Pickering og, Tynan 2, Summerfield
Apr 12th..................Bury (H)..................3-0
Hodges, Tynan 2

KEVIN SUMMERFIELD: SILKY FINISH

NINE STRAIGHT DEFEATS I 1947

IN the interests of keeping things symmetrical, Argyle have experienced a club record nine successive league defeats twice. The first instance straddled two Second Division seasons – 1946/47 and, obviously, 1947/48. Interestingly, neither of them ended in relegation. The first sequence began with a 2-0 home defeat by Birmingham City on April 26th 1947, and ended nigh on five months later, when the Pilgrims drew 0-0 with Leicester City at Home Park. The Birmingham loss set in motion a sequence of six defeats to end the season with, during which Jack Tresadern's Pilgrims conceded 14 goals and scored three. After Birmingham, they went down 2-0 at home to Millwall, and then narrowly lost four successive away matches, at Newport (1-0), Coventry (also 1-0), Bradford Park Avenue (3-2) and, rather spectacularly, Nottingham Forest (5-1). Any thoughts that they might have got things out of their system over the summer break were swiftly shredded on the opening day of the 1947/48 campaign, when Argyle went to Newcastle United and lost 6-1. There followed a second away reverse, at Leicester (2-1) before Birmingham beat them again at Home Park (3-0) to complete the streak they had begun.

Apr 26th .... Birmingham City (H) 0-2
May 3rd .... Millwall (H) 0-2
May 10th .... Newport County (A) 0-1
May 17th .... Coventry City (A) 0-1
May 26th .... Bradford Park Avenue (A) 2-3
R Thomas, Murphy
May 31st .... Nottingham Forest (A) 1-5
R Thomas
Aug 23rd .... Newcastle United (A) 1-6
Tadman
Aug 25th .... Leicester City (A) 1-2
D Thomas
Aug 30th .... Birmingham City (H) 0-3

DON'T HOLD YOUR BREATH

ARGYLE'S 6,000th league goal is due to arrive around 2019 which means that its scorer is probably, at the time of writing, still at primary school.

NINE STRAIGHT DEFEATS II 1963

THE second time Argyle suffered a club record nine straight defeats was also in the Second Division, coming a mere 16 years after the first, but, like the 1947 streak, did not precede a relegation season. The run began at Home Park on October 12th, when Northampton Town cobbled together a convincing 3-0 victory, and did not end until a fortnight before Christmas Day, when two goals from Wilf Carter secured a 2-0 win over Middlesbrough. In between times, as Andy Beattie replaced Ellis Stuttard as manager, the Home Park fortress had been breached by Swindon Town (4-2), Portsmouth (4-0), Norwich City (2-1) and Leeds United (1-0), while the Pilgrims had returned empty-handed from trips to Sunderland (1-0), Rotherham United (3-1), Scunthorpe United (1-0) and Cardiff City (3-1). Statistically similar to the boys from 1947, they managed to score only five goals in the streak but also conceded fewer, 22, as opposed to 25.

Oct 12th .... Northampton Town (H) 0-3
Oct 19th .... Sunderland (A) 0-1
Oct 26th .... Swindon Town (H) 2-4
C Jackson, O'Neill
Nov 2nd .... Rotherham United (A) 1-3
C Jackson
Nov 9th .... Portsmouth (H) 0-4
Nov 16th .... Scunthorpe United (A) 0-1
Nov 23rd .... Norwich City (H) 1-2
Thorne
Nov 30th .... Cardiff City (A) 1-3
Corbett
Dec 7th .... Leeds United (H) 0-1

IT COULD HAVE BEEN YOU

IN 1977, Argyle pioneered a club lottery under marketing man Bill Pearce. The first draw was on September 28th that year and, after 13 draws, Argyle had grossed £130,000. Around £45,000 was paid out in prize-money and spot-gifts of jewellery, furniture and music centres, leaving £58,000 profit.

FIVE STRAIGHT DRAWS I 1929

ARGYLE'S club record win, lose and draw Football League streaks are all quite tidy. While they have twice achieved nine game winnings and losing streaks, their record for consecutive draws – five – has happened four times. The first time they went nap on the shared-honours system came late in the 1928/1929 Third Division (South) season. The sequence for Bob Jack's team started with a 2-2 home draw against Walsall on February 9th 1929, and continued a fortnight later at Home Park with a 1-1 stalemate against Crystal Palace. They achieved the same score at Southend United the following week before a goalless deadlock in the local derby against Exeter City back at home. The string ended on March 11th with another 2-2 result, this time in a midweek match at Luton Town, before a 2-1 defeat at Brighton & Hove Albion brought the five-match drawing streak to an ignominious end.

February 9th .... Walsall (H) 2-2
Black, Matthews
February 23rd .... Crystal Palace (H) 1-1
Matthews
March 2nd .... Southend United (A) 1-1
Bowden
March 9th .... Exeter City (H) 0-0
March 11th .... Luton Town (A) 2-2
Sloan, Leslie

VI AGGRO

'UMBRELLA Vi' was one of the most famous Argyle fans, known for (go on, guess) carrying an umbrella to Home Park in all weathers. Born Violet Pennington, and originally from Eggbuckland, Vi always dressed from top to toe in Argyle colours, and always carried her famous umbrella. When Argyle were promoted to the Second Division in 1986, she was invited on to the balcony of Plymouth Civic Centre during the city's celebrations by manager Dave Smith. She was, naturally, carrying her umbrella. Vi died in November 2002, aged 88. Vi's love of the Greens was not shared by local Plymouth Sound presenter Louise Churchill, who went to a match with her but became upset by the 'unruly' crowd and vowed she would never go to Home Park again.

FIVE STRAIGHT DRAWS II 1997

THERE was a wait of 68 years before Argyle equalled their 'best' for consecutive Football League draws, and then they matched the 1929 effort three times in less than three years. Two of those runs came under the management of Mick Jones, a defender as a player, the first shortly after he succeeded his friend Neil Warnock towards the back end of the 1996/97 Nationwide Second Division season. The run included only two goals as the Pilgrims posted three 0-0s in the five matches. A 1-1 draw at York City on March 29th 1997 kicked things off before Watford were held to a goalless draw at Home Park three days later. The following weekend saw another 1-1 away point, this time at Preston North End, before consecutives 0-0s followed, at home to Stockport County in midweek, and then away at Millwall on the following Saturday. A 2-1 midweek defeat at Notts County ended the share-and-share-alike scenario, but, after two more games, the Pilgrims were back in their spirit of co-operation with the opposition to record another five-game drawing streak.

Mar 29th...................... York City (A) 1-1
Corazzin
Mar 31st .... Watford (H) 0-0
Apr 5th .... Preston North End (A) 1-1
Saunders
Apr 8th .... Stockport County (H) 0-0
Apr 12th .... Millwall (A) 0-0

BUM BALL

ARGYLE striker Sean McCarthy was famously serenaded by Argyle supporters for the size of his ample posterior, but enjoyed the distinction of once scoring for the Pilgrims with that part of his anatomy. Sean scored 47 times for the Greens from 176 games over two spells, including one off his backside. It came in a Nationwide Third Division game at Southend United on September 9th 2000, when he charged down an attempted clearance by the Shrimpers' former Exeter City goalkeeper Andy Woodman. The ball rebounded off Sean's (heck, I'm going to say it) arse for a goal.

FIVE STRAIGHT DRAWS III 1997

THE third time the Pilgrims divvied up the points equally with their opponents for five consecutive Football League games came just three matches after the second time they had done that and spanned the Nationwide Second Division seasons of 1996/97 and 1997/98, after which they were relegated to the Third Division for the second time in their history. The second sorry streak for a Mick Jones team began on May 3rd 1997, when 6,507 people attended Home Park to witness the last rites of a season in which the Pilgrims finished only two spots outside the relegation positions. A 0-0 draw against AFC Bournemouth rather summed things up. The following campaign began with four score-draws, as Argyle briefly assumed the mantle of pools favourites by squaring off at Bristol Rovers (1-1) and Wigan Athletic (also 1-1) and at home to Grimsby Town (2-2) and Chesterfield (1-1 again). The sequence was broken by a 1-0 defeat at home to Watford, and another defeat at Fulham, and two more draws followed before the Pilgrims finally won a game seven weeks into the campaign. Taken in conjunction with the previous five-game drawing streak, the Pilgrims endured a run of 13 successive games, of which they drew ten. For the record, defenders Paul Williams and Mick Heathcote played in all ten games.

May 3rd .... AFC Bournemouth (H) 0-0
Aug 9th .... Bristol Rovers (A) 1-1
Heathcote
Aug 16th .... Grimsby Town (H) 2-2
Logan, Littlejohn
Aug 23rd .... Wigan Athletic (A) 1-1
Logan
Aug 30th .... Chesterfield (H) 1-1
Jean

HARD HARRY

HARRY Roberts made 257 appearances for the Pilgrims at right-back between 1930 and 1937, scoring 21 goals, mainly from the penalty spot. He was not as popular with referees as he was with his team-mates, however, and was often sent off for his tough, rugged and confrontational approach, and, consequently, suspended. When he was serving his enforced absences, his team-mates often held a collection to compensate him for loss of wages.

FIVE STRAIGHT DRAWS IV 2000

TWO seasons after Argyle fans had witnessed a club record five straight Football League draws (or, more accurately, four-fifths of the sequence) the Pilgrims were at it again, this time in the Third Division. The streak began and ended at Home Park, starting on February 26th with a 1-1 sharing of the spoils with Hartlepool United. There followed a winless/unbeaten quartet of matches at Rotherham United (1-1) and Exeter City (also 1-1) and Home Park stalemates against Chester City (0-0) and Lincoln City (1-1). The run of Kevin Hodges' side was broken when Martin Gritton scored the only goal of the game against Cheltenham Town at Home Park on March 18th.

Feb 26th........................ Hartlepool United (H) 1-1
McGregor
Mar 4th......................... Rotherham United (A).................................. 1-1
Hargreaves
Mar 7th......................... Chester City (H) 0-0
Mar 11th....................... Exeter City (A) 1-1
Taylor
Mar 14th....................... Lincoln City (H) 1-1
Barrett

HAVE BOOTS...

MODERN-DAY Pilgrims who moan about the amount of travelling Argyle undertake every season could do worse than consider the example of Matt Middleton, a goalkeeper who represented the Greens before, during and after the Second World War. Middleton joined Argyle from Sunderland in the summer of 1939 and played three Second Division matches before the regular leagues were put on hold because of hostilities. Matt was drafted to work in the coal-mines in Derby, but still managed to play as a guest for Middlesbrough, Carlisle United and Darlington. On top of that, he also played for Argyle when they needed him, often leaving the mines on Friday night and catching the train to play for Argyle the following day before going back to his home in the north. He was probably Argyle's most travelled goalkeeper before Bill Shortt was posted by the army to Plymouth and started playing for Argyle. Middleton was released and went on to play for the cities of Bradford and York.

SIX APPEAL

IN the 1912/13 season, before entering the Football League, Argyle achieved six successive draws in the Southern League, starting with a 1-1 draw against Southampton and ending with the same result at Norwich City.

Feb 21st .... Southampton (H) 1-1
Bowler
Feb 28th .... Reading (A) 2-2
Burch 2
Mar 7th .... Crystal Palace (H) 0-0
Mar 14th .... Coventry City (A) 1-1
Bowler
Mar 21st .... Watford (H) 1-1
Raymond
Mar 28th .... Norwich City (A) 1-1
Burch

THE NAME GAME

PAUL Sturrock's Argyle squad of 2008/09 contained a lot of familiar names: no fewer than 11 of them had names redolent of Pilgrims of the past. Leading scorer Paul Gallagher was preceded by M. Gallagher (1945-46), while fellow strikers Ashley Barnes and Jamie Mackie followed in the studmarks of Bernard Barnes (1955-58) and G. Mackie, a left-sided player who played twice in 1904; Chris Clark was the second C. Clark to play for the Greens, who previously boasted a Charlie Clark (1903-09), as well as a Colin Clarke (1978-79) and a Jimmy Clark (1935-36), and Craig Noone could look back and find Michael Noon (1906-07); midfielder Carl Fletcher was preceded by Charlie Fletcher, who scored six goals in 24 games in 1937-38; first-year pros Lloyd Saxton and Damien McCrory came after Bobby (1967-76) and Sam (1952-55), respectively; Jim Paterson (one T) played at full-back like Mark Patterson (two Ts, 1993-97); Luke Summerfield is the son of Kevin (1984-91), and Dan Smith was the latest in a long line of 'Smudgers' at Home Park. Extending the link to rather long boundaries, Argyle never had a Judge before Alan, although a lot of players have sat on the bench (ouch!), and, if you take former youth-team captain Shane White and mix him with the legendary Sammy Black, you would get David Gray.

THE UNDEFEATED I 1929

THE Pilgrims' record for consecutive undefeated matches can be broken down into two significant streaks. The all-time record, which crossed two seasons, belongs to Robert Jack's Third Division (South) side, while the single-season and post Second World War sequence belongs to fellow Scot Paul Sturrock's Nationwide Third Division champions of 2001/02. Jack's men strung together the high-water mark of 22 games without defeat between April 20th and December 21st 1929. The run began four games from the end of the 1928/29 season, which saw the Pilgrims finish fourth in the table, when they beat Luton Town 2-0 at Home Park, courtesy of two Sammy Black goals. The final three games of the campaign also ended 2-0, away at Brentford, and home to both Bristol Rovers and Bournemouth & Boscombe Athletic. The Greens made it five 2-0s in succession four months later on the opening day of the 1929/30 season – in which they gained promotion having never finished outside the top four in the Third Division (South) table for ten seasons – by beating Clapton Orient in London. They made it all the way to Christmas Day without being beaten, winning at Torquay United (4-3), Bristol Rovers (3-2), Watford (2-0), Swindon Town (2-1) and drawing on their travels at Northampton Town, Southend United and Bournemouth & Boscombe Athletic (1-1); giving out Home Park beatings to Torquay United (5-0), Gillingham (3-0), Exeter City (4-1), Merthyr Town (2-1) Luton Town (6-1), Fulham (3-1), and Crystal Palace (6-1), and drawing at home with Brentford, Brighton & Hove Albion and Walsall (all 1-1). The streak was busted on December 25th when they lost 1-0 at Coventry City, but the Greens immediately gained a small manner of revenge by beating the Sky Blues 24 hours later in the Boxing Day return at Home Park. Argyle scored 56 goals in the 22 matches, conceding 17 in reply. The goals were shared around: Ray Bowden scored in 13 of the games, collecting 15 in total including a never-have-to-buy-a-drink-again hat-trick against Exeter City; Sammy Black hit 12; Jack Leslie nine; and Tommy Grozier seven, including four against Crystal Palace; Jack Vidler scored four; Jack Pullen and Frank Sloan two; and Norman Mackay, Fred McKenzie and Freddy Forbes one each. The missing goal was netted by goalkeeper Fred Craig, who vacated his penalty area to stride forward to net a party-piece goal from the penalty spot at Torquay – the only game in the sequence when the Pilgrims conceded more than twice.

THE UNDEFEATED II – 2001

WHAT is it about Argyle and Christmas time? The modern era and one-season club record for consecutive league matches without defeat also went up the Swanee just before the 2001 festive season, three games shy of the all-time record set 62 years earlier. Paul Sturrock's Nationwide Third Division title-winners started on their march to the record books on Bank Holiday Monday, August 27th when, having experienced three defeats and a draw from their opening four games, they came from behind to win 3-2 at Rushden & Diamonds. It was not until December 22nd, when they visited Scunthorpe and lost 2-1, that they tasted a league defeat again. Their first Home Park win was not until September 11th, when, in naturally sombre circumstances, they beat Swansea City. That was followed by wins against Macclesfield Town (2-0), Luton Town (2-1), Halifax Town (3-0), Lincoln City (2-0), Hartlepool United (1-0), Carlisle United (3-0), and Darlington (1-0); away victories at Torquay United (1-0), Exeter City (3-2), Mansfield Town (3-0), Bristol Rovers (2-1), and Southend United (1-0); and on-the-road points from games at Kidderminster Harriers (0-0), York City (0-0), Oxford United (1-1), Cheltenham Town (0-0), and Leyton Orient (0-0). Rushden & Diamonds were the only side to score more than once against the Pilgrims during the run and 13 sides did not score at all. The 31 goals scored by Argyle were shared around with fewer than a third coming from recognised strikers Michael Evans (four), Nicky Banger (two), and Ian Stonebridge (two). Frenchman David Friio (seven) was leading scorer, and fellow midfielders Buster Phillips (six), Lee Hodges (three), Steve Adams (one) and Jason Bent (one), also chipped in. Central defender Graham Coughlan, who finished the campaign as the club's top scorer, netted thrice and club captain Paul Wotton and full-back Brian McGlinchey scored one each.

FACE TO FACE

ARGYLE striker Dwight Marshall did not have a happy day at the Deva Stadium during the 1998/99 Third Division season, despite notching one of his 48 goals for the Pilgrims. Not only did Argyle lose 3-2 to Chester City on March 27th, Dwight was injured immediately after scoring his goal… when one of the Green Army celebrated rather too enthusiastically with him, and smashed Dwight in the face with his head.

DWIGHT MARSHALL: SMASHING FELLOW

UNLUCKY THIRTEEN

NINETEEN sixty-three was undoubtedly not the best time to be an Argyle fan. Not only did the Pilgrims equal an all-time low for successive league defeats – nine, between October 12th and December 7th – they also set another club record for consecutive league matches without a win – 13; a run that had ended only ten days before the defeat streak began. The run spanned two Second Division seasons, beginning with a 3-0 reverse at Luton Town in the second-last game of the 1962-63 campaign, and two managers – Ellis Stuttard and Andy Beattie – before the Greens next tasted victory in a 3-2 Home Park success over Grimsby Town in their 12th game of the 1963/64 season on October 5th. After Luton, the Pilgrims went down 2-1 to Cardiff City in the season-closer at Ninian Park. They drew the first home match of the new season 2-2 with Leyton Orient. There followed Home Park defeats by Newcastle United (4-3) and Preston North End (2-0); draws at home to Derby County (0-0) and Sunderland (1-1), away losses at Leyton Orient (1-0), Huddersfield, (4-3) and Charlton Athletic (1-0); and draws at Preston North End (0-0) and Bury (2-2) before the Mariners sailed into choppy waters. There was just time to squeeze out a creditable 1-1 draw at Manchester City before the start of the nine-game losing streak, which meant that the Pilgrims managed just the Grimsby win in a sequence of 24 consecutive league games. Remarkably, they stayed up that season. On goal average. From Grimsby.

SWEET CHERRETT

PERCY Cherrett, who scored 37 Third Division goals for Argyle between 1923 and 1925, netted in six consecutive games between December 1st and 26th 1923. Remarkably, in the last five of them, he was on a hat-trick but never went on to claim the match-ball… in those matches or, for Argyle, ever. Percy's run began in inauspicious circumstances on December 1st with a single goal in a 3-2 defeat at Queens Park Rangers. The following week, the fixture was reversed, as was the result, with Argyle winning 2-0 and Percy netting both. In the subsequent four victories – 2-1 at Newport; 3-2 against Newport at Home Park; and 4-0 successes over Exeter City at home, first, and then away, Percy scored twice, giving him a total of 11 goals in six successive matches.

MAURICE MAJOR

MAURICE Tadman scored ten goals in five successive Third Division matches between October 7th and November 4th 1950, as the Pilgrims went goal crazy. First, they beat Torquay United 3-1 at Plainmoor, with Tadman scoring twice; then they beat Aldershot 5-1 at home, with Tadman scoring four. A 2-1 victory at Swindon Town followed, Tadman again netting; before Colchester were thrashed 7-1 at Home Park (Tadman 2, Strauss 2, Govan, Dews, Dougall). Tadman made it double-figures in the subsequent match, at Bristol Rovers, which the Pilgrims lost 3-1.

LOAN STAR

ON the subject of hot goalscoring streaks, special mention should be given to Argyle legend Tommy Tynan, who returned to Home Park on loan from Rotherham United at the end of the 1985/86 season – having joined the Millers from Argyle the previous summer. He scored ten in eight matches to help win promotion to the Second Division. Tommy drew a blank in his first game back, a 3-1 win at Bournemouth, but did score two on his return to Home Park, a 4-0 win against Rotherham! They had omitted to include any clause in the loan agreement about not being able to play against your parent club. Seeing as Tommy had fallen out with Millers' boss Norman Hunter, it is doubtful he felt any remorse about his double. On the subject of doubles, Tommy scored two more in the next match, a 3-0 home win against Bury, and netted the point-winner in a 1-1 draw at Lincoln City. A 3-0 reverse for the Pilgrims at Wigan briefly threatened to derail their promotion campaign before consecutive home wins against Bolton Wanderers, 4-1, and Blackpool, 3-1, in which Tommy scored, was followed by the conclusive 4-0 Home Park win against Bristol City (Tynan 2, Nelson, Coughlin). For good measure, Argyle finished the campaign with a 2-0 win at Darlington, Tynan fittingly scoring the final goal of the promotion-winning season.

HORNETS' STING

THE Pilgrims were FA Cup semi-finalists for the only time in their history in 1983/84, having beaten Southend United, Barking, Newport County, Darlington, Derby County and West Bromwich Albion. John Hore's Third Division side lost 1-0 to Watford at Villa Park.

QUICK CHADWICK

ARGYLE'S quickest goal was scored on December 17th 2005 when Nick Chadwick sent the Pilgrims on their way to a 2-0 Championship victory against Crystal Palace after only 11.83 seconds of the game. Argyle only took five touches as they went from 0-0 to 1-0, the kick-off being touched back to Mathias Kouo-Doumbe, whose long ball forward was headed on by Michael Evans for Chadwick to lob the ball over the disastrously out-of-position goalkeeper Julian Speroni. Argyle's second that day came from Tony Capaldi, in the fourth minute of injury time. There has surely never been a greater time difference between two consecutive Argyle goals.

MACKIE THE KNIFE

JAMIE Mackie scored the quickest debut goal in Argyle history when he netted within 11 seconds of coming on as substitute in a 3-0 Championship victory over Barnsley on February 12th 2008; Mackie's 76th-minute strike was a full 52 seconds quicker than Tony Witter's headed opening goal in the 2-2 home draw with Leicester City on January 11th 1992. Central defender Witter, who was on loan to David Kemp's Argyle from QPR, nodded in a corner at the Devonport end in the second minute of the Barclays Second Division match with his first touch in senior competitive football. However, Mackie is way outside the quickest debut strike of all time, which appears to belong to Brendan O'Callaghan, who scored in his first appearance for Stoke City. He was a 75th-minute substitute, like Mackie, in a home match against Hull City on March 8th 1978. Stoke were waiting to take a corner when he came on and went straight to the penalty area and headed home the cross. In game-time, he had not been on the pitch for more than three seconds.

GALL ON

THE fastest goal scored by an Argyle player away from Home Park also belongs in the modern era. It came on February 28th 2009 and was scored by Paul Gallagher in a Championship game at Wolverhampton Wanderers. The goal was timed at 38 seconds, beating the previous quickest goal ever scored by an Argyle player in an away match – Terry Austin's opener in a 2-2 draw at Lincoln City on January 2nd 1978 – by a full 14 seconds.

DAN'S THE MAN

ANOTHER notable quick strike in Argyle's history went to Marino Keith, who scored after 29 seconds of the home game against Bristol Rovers on March 30th 2002, the match after the Pilgrims had sealed promotion to the Nationwide Second Division. The goal was nearly even quicker as Keith converted a loose ball after a shot from Steve Adams had hit the crossbar. There were no more goals in the match.

FAST GUYS

ANOTHER quickie was John Mitten's opener in a Second Division game at home to Derby County on January 20th 1968. Mitten ties with Paul Gallagher in joint third on the fastest goals chart, netting after 38 seconds of the 4-3 defeat by the Rams. Martin Gritton netted in the first minute in a 1-1 Third Division draw at Brighton & Hove Albion on February 12th 2000.

WHO'S WHO?

TONY Witter played only three games for the Pilgrims in their relegation season of 1991/92 but they could hardly be said to be uneventful. As well as scoring with his first touch as a senior professional, Witter was involved in one of the most bizarre bookings in Pilgrims' history. Having committed a foul deemed worthy of a yellow card, Witter turned round to find the referee booking team-mate Tony Spearing instead. Mistaken identity issues are not that rare in football, but Witter was 6ft plenty and black, while the team-mate who was mistaken for him, Tony Spearing was about six inches shorter and white. To compound the error, the official called Spearing 'skipper' when he was being cautioned. Argyle's captain that day was Jock Morrison, a man hewn from Aberdonian granite and twice as big as the diminutive Spearing.

FALTY SCREBARD

HOME Park once boasted an electronic scoreboard, situated at the back of the old Barn Park terracing. The omens for the new technology were not good when, on its 1986 launch, it did not work at first, and then caught fire. It continued to be of more value on match days for its comedy element than its usefulness (wrong scores, missing letters, etc.) and lasted just two seasons.

CARD CAPER

TERRY Fleming and Tony Dennis, Argyle players of different vintages, were involved in a booking nightmare when they were Lincoln City teammates. Fleming, who played 23 matches for Argyle between 2000 and 2001, was booked by referee Paul Taylor in the first half of Lincoln's match against Wigan Athletic at Sincil Bank in February 1997. Eight minutes later, he committed another foul which saw Taylor produce another card. To everyone's amazement, the card was yellow, with no red following. It turned out that Fleming had given Taylor the name of Dennis, a former Argyle trainee who played 10 times for the Greens between 1981 and 1983, instead of his own. Fleming was charged with bringing the game into disrepute, disciplined by Lincoln, and still got a three-match ban.

ARGYLE PLAYERS OF THE SEASON

CANADIAN international Giancarlo Michele Corazzin, better known to his team-mates and the Green Army as 'Carlo', was the first overseas player to win the Argyle Player of the Season award. Or, more accurately, to share it. Carlo, who scored 24 goals in 86 appearances for Argyle between 1996 and 1998, was a half-recipient of the annual gong in 1998, along with stalwart Pilgrim Martin Barlow. No doubt the award was tainted by the fact that Argyle were relegated to the Nationwide Third Division, going into the lowest tier of the English game for only the second time in their history. Corazzin and Barlow were in the team that lost 2-1 against Burnley on the final day of the 1997/98 campaign in a loser-goes-down game at Turf Moor; Corazzin and six others – not including Barlow – left in the summer.

REF! REF!

ARGYLE played Portsmouth in the Golden Jubilee Dockyard Derby match on May 4th 1953. The game was unusual in that it trialled the oft-mooted idea of having two referees, one in each half of the pitch, the idea being that it would be easier for the officials to keep up with play. D. L. Scoble, from Plymouth, was one referee, and Jack Wiltshire, from Torpoint, was the other. Argyle ran out winners, with Alex Govan getting the only goal of the game, but there must have been pitfalls because nothing subsequently came of the experimental system.

CROOKES IN THE BOARDROOM

SOME chairmen are often accused by fans of being crooks (though never at Home Park), and Argyle have had one who can hold his hands up to the fact (sort of): C. W. Crookes, who briefly stepped up to the plate in the late 1960s between the Stafford Williams reign and Robert Daniel's second stint in the hot seat. The longest serving of the 19 chairmen who have served Argyle was Sir Clifford Tozer, who was in charge of the club for 19 years from 1938-1957; E. Elliot-Square, who sounds more like an address, than a director, had previously taken control for 16 years between 1919 and 1935; and Robert Daniel was top banana for 16 years, initially between 1964-65, and then 1968 to 1983. At the other end of the spectrum, B. Spooner, Clarence N. Spooner and Capt. F. Windrum held the chair for a combined period of four years only. The 17th chairman, Paul Stapleton, was voted to the number one post by his fellow directors in 2001.

THE ARGYLE CHAIRMEN

1903-1905 .... B. Spooner
1905-1906 .... Clarence N. Spooner
1906-1907 .... Capt F. Windrum
1907-1910 .... R. F. Davis
1910-1915 .... Stanley Spooner
1915-1919 .... War years
1919-1935 .... E Elliot-Square
1935-1938 .... Lt. Col T. McCready
1938-1957 .... Sir Clifford Tozer
1957-1964 .... Ron Blindell
1964-1965 .... Robert Daniel
1965-1967 .... Stafford Williams
1967-1968 .... C. W. Crookes
1968-1983 .... Robert Daniel
1983-1985 .... Stuart Dawe
1985-1991 .... Peter D. Bloom
1991-2001 .... Dan McCauley
2001- .... Paul Stapleton

THIRD DIVISION WORLD CHAMPIONS

PRE-SEASON tours for Argyle had, up until the latter part of the 20th century normally meant a quick jaunt around Devon and Cornwall to play local sides. The first overseas tour came before the 1924/25 season, when they visited South America for a nine-game, five-week trip that did not end until a few days before the beginning of the subsequent campaign. The Argyle Handbook of 1954/55 records that: "At the conclusion of the tour, Mr. Bob Jack declared that the standard of South American football was higher than he had anticipated to find and was quite equal to Third Division standard at home." Six years after his comments, Uruguay won the World Cup.

SLOPING OFF

THE pitch at Home Park is 110 x 72 yards, and it is not flat, but slopes from the centre of the pitch towards the corners.

FESTIVE OCCASIONS

ARGYLE'S first match on Christmas Day was in 1903, when they lost 1-0 to Reading in a Southern League match at Home Park. The last time the Pilgrims played on Christmas Day was in 1957, when they beat Newport County 2-0 in a Third Division (South) game in front of 10,680 festive Welsh souls. Tom Baker (who was not a doctor) and Jimmy Gauld netted. The following day, the two teams resumed hostilities at Home Park, where 25,936 people donned their new cardies to see the Pilgrims win for the second successive day, Wilf Carter scoring the only goal of the match. The last time Argyle played a home game on Christmas Day had been six years previously, when Bristol City were the visitors for a Third Division (South) match. The game, watched by 17,498, followed the sharing nature of the season in a 2-2 draw. Peter Rattray scored both Argyle's goals.

FIRST SUNDAY

THE first Sunday match at Home Park was not until December 20th 1987 (a Christmas shopping-influenced decision), when Bradford City were the visitors. Argyle won 2-1; Steve Cooper and Mark Smith scored; and 11,350 people savoured the new experience.

STEVE COOPER (WATCHED BY SECRETARY GRAHAM LITTLE AND MANAGER DAVE SMITH): SUNDAY SCORER

THE CZAR OF HOME PARK

ARGYLE chairman Ron Blindell was not a wealthy businessman for nothing, and his eye for the main chance was acute in the winter of the 1961/62 season. First, Home Park became the centre of attention of the British, not to say world, media when it hosted what would have been an unremarkable reserve team game between the Pilgrims and Tottenham Hotspur were it not for the fact that the match represented Jimmy Greaves' first game back in Blighty after his unsuccessful Italian sojourn. A crowd of more than 12,000 saw Greavesie score in a 4-2 Combination League win for Spurs, but not before Blindell had addressed the masses through the PA system. "On behalf of Plymouth Argyle, Devon, Cornwall and last, but not least, the whole of England, I say to you welcome. We are glad to have you back." At least he had his locations in the right order. Six weeks later, Blindell Productions were out in full force when Spurs visited Home Park again, this time in the fourth round of the FA Cup. This time, Second Division Argyle were no match for the cup-holders, who contained not only Greaves, but also Cliff Jones, Danny Blanchflower, John White and Dave Mackay, and won 5-1. The crowd was 40,040 and they had been well entertained. Blindell, revelling in his affectionate nickname of the Czar of Home Park, saw the opportunity for the club to improve its financial position, and arranged for the gates and all the club bars to be open at noon. He put on attractive pre-match entertainment, including an army band, an RAF police-dog team, and, to give it that Wembley feeling, community singing.

THE THOUGHTS OF CHAIRMAN RON

RON Blindell, Argyle chairman between 1957 and 1964, was a man of opinions. Not all of which were shared by the rest of the footballing world. Chairman Ron once proposed that: players should have only two weeks' holiday a year; players should work hours more comparable to industry and business; what he called "this nonsense" of a close season should be done away with; and that football should abandon a basic wage and reserve-team wage – instead, each player would be expected to do "an honest day's work for an honest day's pay". It will surprise you not at all that Ron's plan was condemned by PFA secretary Cliff Lloyd.

TOURING CYCLE

IT was not until 1954 that Argyle set out on their second pre-season tour, this time to the USA, for ten games in 44 days. They travelled 14,000 miles by sea, air and land. Nine years later, Argyle went on a four-game trip behind the Iron Curtain, playing in Poland and East Germany. In 1997, Argyle visited Gambia at the end of the season for a jolly… sorry, important cultural exchange visit and a game against the Africans' national team, which Argyle won 2-1. The most expensive seats in the ground cost only 10 dalasi, about 70p. With the arrival of Paul Sturrock in 2000, pre-season tours became the norm, a tradition that was carried on by Bobby Williamson, Tony Pulis and Ian Holloway. Scotland, Austria and Sweden have been the destinations of choice.

1924	South America
1954	United States
1963	Eastern Europe
1965	Germany
1967	Holland-Germany
1969	Southern Ireland
1974	France
1981	France
1990	Sweden
1997	Gambia
2001	Scotland
2002	Scotland
2003	Austria
2004	Austria
2005	Sweden
2006	Austria
2007	Austria
2008	Austria

CHARLIE CALLING

ARGYLE pre-first world war defender Charlie Clark handed out his own postcard-type calling-cards.

ELECTRICS TO PASTIES

SINCE shirt-sponsorship has been permitted by the authorities, seven different names have adorned the chests of the Pilgrims' players, ranging from an electrical superstore, through a couple of insurance companies and a pair of newspapers, to the manufacturers of perhaps the country's most well-known Cornish pasty. Argyle's initial shirt sponsors, in 1983/84, were Beacon Electrical. The following two years saw the name of Ivor Jones' Insurance on the front of the Green. Ivor later became a director of the club. After two years, National & Provincial had the honour for a season, before the *Sunday Independent* newspaper began a five-year stint on the chests. They were succeeded by chairman Dan McCauley's Rotolok company – "manufacturers of rotary airlocks and complementary powder and bulk solid handling technologies", in case you were wondering – for six years before the *Plymouth Evening Herald* (as it was then) enjoyed a four-year spell advertising their product. In 2002, Ginsters took over for what has proved to be the longest association between Argyle and any shirt sponsor.

1983-84	Beacon Electrical
1984-86	Ivor Jones
1986-87	National & Provincial
1987-92	Sunday Independent
1992-98	Rotolok
1998-02	Evening Herald
2002-09	Ginsters

JUMBO TALES

'JUMBO' Jack Chisholm was a giant of a man, who had no cartilages and liked a drink, but nevertheless (or maybe 'because of that'?) has achieved legendary status at Home Park, even being voted into the Pilgrims' Team of the Century. He began his career at Tottenham Hotspur, and arrived at Argyle by way of Brentford and Sheffield United in December 1949. He made his debut in a 2-1 home Second Division victory over Chesterfield on Christmas Eve 1949, and stayed four and half years at Home Park, leading the side out of the Third Division (South) in 1952 before retiring through injury. He played 187 games for Argyle, often inspirationally, never unnoticeably.

KITTED OUT

IN the modern era, Argyle's kit has been supplied by 11 different manufacturers, including their own, ranging from Umbro to adidas, and including such iconic brands as Puma, Bukta and Admiral.

> 1975-1976...Umbro
> 1976-1978.. Pilgrim
> 1978-1980..Bukta
> 1980-1982... adidas
> 1982-1987.. Pilgrim
> 1987-1990...Umbro
> 1990-1991.. Ribero
> 1992-1996...Admiral
> 1995-1997..................................Super League
> 1998-1999...Errea
> 1999-2003.. Patrick
> 2003-2005..TFG
> 2005-2009...Puma

RAINED OFF

THE first recorded abandonment of a match at Home Park came on January 14th 1939 in a Second Division game against Norwich City. The game was called off in the second half because heavy rain had made the pitch unplayable, with Argyle leading 1-0 through John Archer's 14th-minute goal. The match was eventually replayed on May 3rd, when – with nice synchronicity – Argyle won 1-0, through a Dave Thomas goal. Archer did not play in the game. More recently, a similar set of circumstances saw Argyle again frustrated. With the Pilgrims leading 1-0 in a home Championship game against Leicester City on November 1st 2005, referee Andy Woolmer deemed the pitch unplayable at half-time because of heavy rain. The decision disappointed Argyle manager Tony Pulis – "The players are paid a lot of money today to play football in different conditions; I didn't see any tackle that would put any player in any danger at all; I didn't see any slip into anyone or fall over" – and Chadwick, who had waited since the opening day of the season to score. The match was replayed a few months later, when Argyle won 1-0, although Paul Wotton, and not Chadwick, scored the decisive goal.

TERRIER-ISED

BETWEEN September 7th and January 11th of the 1963/64 season, Argyle played Huddersfield Town six times… and did not win a single game. They were knocked out of both cup competitions by the Yorkshire side and picked up just one point from the two league meetings between them. The sorry sequence began at Leeds Road on September 7th 1963, when the Pilgrims went down by the odd goal in seven, Duncan Neale, Wilf Carter, and Alan O'Neill scoring. A little over two weeks later, a League Cup saga began at Home Park, where the first-round tie ended all square at 2-2, with Alex Jackson scoring Argyle's two. No sudden-death penalty shoot-outs in those days, so it was back to Leeds Road three weeks later for a replay which could not separate the teams as the game ended 3-3. Ken Maloy, Johnny Williams and Jimmy McAnearney rang in the Pilgrims' triple. A week later, they locked horns again, this time at the neutral venue of Villa Park – where only 3,000 people turned up to see Huddersfield prevail at the third time of asking, 2-1. Maloy scored again for Argyle. After this marathon, which was watched by fewer than 15,000 people in total, imagine the unconfined joy there must have been when the third-round draw of the FA Cup handed Argyle a plum home time against… you guessed. Huddersfield won 1-0. A week later, it was just like déjà vu all over again when Argyle entertained (I use the word loosely) the Terriers in a league match. The 0-0 scoreline could have reflected that familiarity with each other's strengths and weaknesses meant that they cancelled each other out. Or it could have been that they were pretty well bored to death with playing each other.

WHITE STUFF

THE first time the Pilgrims used a white ball was on January 10th 1953 against Coventry City in a third-round FA Cup match. The referee called for it ten minutes from the end of the game, on a need-to-see basis, in spite of the match having kicked off at 2.15pm. Despite Coventry scoring in the sixth minute, Argyle won 4-1, with George Dews, Arthur Smith, Gordon Astall, and Alex Govan all netting. Notably, all the goals came in the first half, and each side had a penalty saved by the opposition goalkeeper.

OFF THE CHARTS

THE first recorded song by a Plymouth Argyle squad was It's A Long Way To Plymouth Argyle with music backing by the Mount Charles Silver Band, St Austell, in 1975. While it would certainly not lose marks for truthfulness (although I guess how far it is to Plymouth Argyle rather depends on your starting point: it's not that far from Saltash, for example, but a bit of a slog if you live in Vienna), it lost out on originality, it simply being a re-working of the old war time classic It's A Long Way To Tipperary. Given a choice of buying the Pilgrims' efforts, brought out to coincide with promotion to the Second Division, or I'm Not in Love by 10CC, Johnny Nash's Tears On My Pillow, or even Barbados by Typically Tropical, it was no contest for the trendy young things of the Westcountry, and It's A Long Way To Plymouth Argyle remained a long way off charting.

I SPY...

BERNARD Barnes, a centre-forward who made six appearances for the Pilgrims between 1955 and 1958, scoring three goals, wore glasses. It is not known whether any referees asked to borrow them during a game – or whether he offered to lend them to any officials.

BIG MAC TRIPLE

ARGYLE players have scored a hat-trick in a Devon Derby on only seven occasions – two against Exeter City and five against Torquay United. The last Pilgrim to score three times in a little local spat was Paul McGregor, who performed the feat in a Third Division clash against Torquay United at Plainmoor on March 25th 2000. It is the only time an Argyle player has rung in a triple in a Devon Derby at a venue other than Home Park. The other hat-tricksters against the Gulls are Adrian Littlejohn, who achieved his three in a 4-3 home win in Neil Warnock's 1995/95 Nationwide Third Division promotion-winning season, on October 23rd; Mike Bickle, who hit four in a 6-0 Third Division victory on Boxing Day 1969; and Percy Richards, who boosted his headwear collection by two little more than a year by notching successive Third Division (South) hat-tricks on March 17th 1928 and March 29th 1929, games which the Pilgrims won 4-1 and 4-0 respectively.

RAY OF SUNSHINE

MORE than 80 seasons have passed since a Pilgrim last scored a hat-trick against Exeter City, a feat which has been performed only twice. Jack Fowler did it first in a Third Division (South) encounter on March 30th 1923, which Argyle won 5-1, and Ray Bowden matched his effort in a 4-1 Third Division (South) beating on October 26th 1928 in what was quite an era for hat-tricks. Since then, the only man to register three goals in an Argyle-Exeter encounter is Johnny Nicholls, who achieved the feat in a Third Division (South) game on February 8th 1958, when Argyle lost 4-2 to the team that finished bottom of the table that campaign. Had Argyle won, they would have been crowned the 1957/58 champions. Nicholls, an FA Cup winner with West Bromwich Albion in the 1954 FA Cup Final, won two England caps before joining Exeter in 1957.

WESTCOUNTRY HAT-TRICK PILGRIMS

March 30th 1923 ....Jack Fowler ....Argyle 5 Exeter 1
March 17th 1928 ....Percy Richards.............Argyle 4 Torquay 1
March 29th 1929 ....Percy Richards.............Argyle 4 Torquay 0
October 26th 1928...............Ray Bowden ....Argyle 4 Exeter 1
December 26th 1969 ....Mike Bickle ....Argyle 6 Torquay 0
October 23rd 1995...............Adie Littlejohn............Argyle 4 Torquay 3
March 25th 2000 ....Paul McGregor ....Torquay 0 Argyle 4

FOUR TIMES SEVEN

THE Pilgrims' meaningless 8-1 victory at Hartlepool United on the final day of the 1993/94 season also represents their largest winning margin in an away game. They have also won by seven goals three further times, all at Home Park; the 8-1 triumph over Millwall in 1932, and two 7-0 wins. The first of these was on September 5th 1936, when Doncaster Rovers suffered at the hands of Jackie Smith (3), Jack Vidler (2), Sammy Black and Jimmy Hunter. The second came in the opening week of 2004, on January 3rd, when David Friio (3), Nathan Lowndes (2), Lee Hodges and Tony Capaldi scored in a Nationwide Second Division game against Chesterfield.

FIRST FOOTYING

HOW important is it to win the first match of the season? Looking at the Pilgrims' promotion seasons, the answer appears to be "not very". Take the two most recent promotion seasons, for example: Argyle were promoted as Nationwide Third Division champions at the end of the 2001-02 season with a whopping 102 points, but only after they had an awful start, losing at home to Shrewsbury; drawing at Hull; losing a League Cup tie to Watford; and losing at home again, to Rochdale. Again, in 2003/04, the Pilgrims were promoted, to the Championship, as champions, having not won any of their first three matches. An opening-day draw at home to Grimsby Town, was followed by defeat at Colchester United in the Carling Cup, and a league loss to Rushden & Diamonds. Here is a summary of all promotion seasons:

1929/30: Third Division (South) champions. Won the first match of the season, at Clapton Orient, and did not lose until Christmas Day.
1951/52: Third Division (South) champions. Lost the first match at Orient.
1958/59: Third Division champions. Drew first match 1-1 at Hull City.
1974/75: Promoted after coming second in the Second Division. Lost first match 1-0 at Preston North End.
1985/86: Promoted after coming second in the Second Division. Lost first two matches, 3-1 at York City and 1-0 at home to Reading.
1995/96: Promoted via the Third Division play-offs. Lost the first six matches of the season.
2001/02: Third Division champions. Lost the first three league matches.
2003/04: Second Division champions. Lost the first two league matches.

LIKE BUSES

PETER Gilbert scored only twice in 84 appearances for the Pilgrims between 2003 and 2005. No surprise there, considering that, as left-back, his prime job was to help keep goals out. What was notable about his two goals was the fact that they came in the same week of his two-year stay at Home Park, both in front of the home fans. The first was the third in a 6-0 thrashing of Tranmere Rovers in a Nationwide Second Division game on October 11th 2003; the second was the fourth in a 4-0 LDV Vans Trophy drubbing of Westcountry rivals Bristol City three days later.

PAID IN FULL

WHEN Jumbo Jack Chisholm was captain of the Pilgrims in the early 1950s, there was never a dull moment. Just before one Christmas, some Pilgrims wanted to buy presents for their children, and some – to use a naval term – wanted 'a run ashore'. Jack knew some of them were a bit short of cash, but, being the captain, went along to see manager Jimmy Rae and asked if the players could be paid their win bonus for their match against Torquay United. Jimmy was a bit puzzled and checked his fixture-list before informing Jack that, since the game had not been played, that would not be possible. Jack replied that he knew the game was still to be played, but, as Argyle always beat the Gulls, could the players be paid in advance? Jimmy saw it from Jack's point of view and agreed to it! Jack won that day and Argyle, as promised, won the match.

EYE OFF THE BALL

DAVE Smith, Argyle manager in the mid-1980s, was a 'do the routine' type of manager, and often made the half-time tea as he prepared his mid-game team talk. At a Barclays Second Division game at Reading in August 1987, the self-styled 'Ciderman' exited the dug-out a minute before the interval to put the kettle on in the Elm Park away dressing-room. In doing so, he missed an Argyle goal. In fairness, there was not a very big cheer because there were not many away fans and, it was an own goal from future Exeter City manager Gary Peters. Nobody thought to mention the goal to Dave, so he did his half-time team talk, went back to the dug-out after the interval, and spent the whole of the second half thinking the Pilgrims were hanging on for a draw. After the match, with no more goals – seen or unseen – chief coach Martin Harvey mentioned that, although it was early in the season, the Pilgrims must have been in a good position in the league table. Smithy said that one point would not have pushed Argyle up very far. The penny dropped for Harve, who realised what must have happened and told Smithy Argyle had secured three points. Smithy was bewildered at first and then saw the funny side of it. More importantly, Argyle went top of the table with those three points.

DAVE SMITH: NOT THE BEST PERSON TO CHECK YOUR POOLS COUPON

EIGHT HAUL

THE highest number of goals Argyle have scored in one league match is eight, a total they have achieved on three different occasions. The first was on January 16th 1932 when they beat Millwall 8-1 in a Third Division (South) game at Home Park. Jack Vidler led the way with a hat-trick, and Ray Bowden netted a couple, with other goals coming from Jack Leslie, Sammy Black and an own goal. The second time was also at home, against Mansfield Town in their Third Division title-winning season of 1958/59, and the 8-3 victory remains the highest number of aggregate goals witnessed by a Home Park crowd in a single match. Five Argyle players scored, with Johnny Williams grabbing two and Alex Govan, Harry Penk, Jimmy Gauld and Wilf Carter also scoring. Those of you totting up as you go along will be wondering where the other two goals came from. Well, they were generously contributed by Mansfield centre-half Terry Swinscoe, in one of only 14 appearances for the Stags. The previous week, the Pilgrims had lost 4-2 at home to Accrington Stanley. Who? Exactly. The third occasion Argyle hit eight – and the only time they have done it at a ground other than Home Park – was as recently as May 7th 1994, when they beat Hartlepool United 8-1 in an Endsleigh Third Division game. Watched by just 2,382 people, and needing to win to have any chance of promotion, the Pilgrims scored through Richard Landon (3), Paul Dalton (2), Dwight Marshall, Steve McCall and Steve Castle. No oggies this time. It was all in vain, however, as Port Vale won at Brighton & Hove Albion on the same afternoon to pip the Pilgrims to the Second Division.

SIX SHOOTERS

ARGYLE have twice been hit for six at Home Park. Their worst ever home defeat occurred on August 25th 1956, when they were turned over 6-0 by Reading in their second Third Division (South) game of the season at Home Park. The goalkeeper was Dyer, although this appears to be his name, rather than a description of his performance. Incidentally, the Greens finished just two places lower than the Royals (or the Biscuitmen, as they were more widely known in those days) in the final table. Twenty-five years earlier, the Pilgrims had suffered their first, and only other, six-goal beating at Home Park, by those giants of the game, Bury, losing 6-3 in a Second Division game on January 3rd 1931.

VICTORIA GRIND

THE pièce de résistance in the Greens running up the white flag came at the Victoria Ground, Stoke-on-Trent, on December 17th 1960 (what is it about Argyle, Christmas, and bad results?) when the Pilgrims capitulated to their worst ever league defeat in a Second Division game – although 'game' implies some sort of involvement that the 9-0 scoreline did not immediately indicate (remember on the *Grandstand* tele/video-printer when that happened and the inputter used to type 'NINE' in full as confirmation that your eyes were not deceiving you?). For the Hall of Shame only, the Argyle team that day was: Geoff Barnsley, George Robertson, Bryce Fulton, Johnny Williams, Gordon Fincham, Johnny Newman, Peter Anderson, Jimmy McAnearney, Alex Jackson, Wilf Carter, Ken Maloy, which, on the face of it, does not look a bad line-up, does it?

UNHAPPY CHRISTMAS

IT was not the happiest Christmas for Argyle in 1930, and certainly one of the most up and down festive periods. As well as suffering one of their heaviest home defeats at the hands of Bury (6-3), they also notched up one of their heaviest away trouncings when, on December 27th, they went down 9-1 at Everton in a Second Division game, the first of only two occasions in which they have shipped nine goals. Bizarrely, the Greens had registered impressive wins in the games preceding the two thrashings, beating Cardiff City 5-1 at Home Park the day before their Goodison rout, and winning 4-0 at Barnsley in the only match played between the Everton and Bury defeats.

BAD-ISON PARK

REMARKABLY, Argyle's 9-1 thrashing at Everton in 1930 is not the highest-scoring away game in which they have been involved. Even more remarkably, it is not even the highest-scoring away game at Goodison in which they have been involved. That honour – and the honour of the Argyle league game in which most goals have been scored – goes to the Second Division match between the two sides on February 27th 1954, which ended Everton 8 (EIGHT) Argyle 4. The Pilgrims' contribution to the goalfest came from debutant Neil Langman (2), Malcolm Davies and Sam McCrory.

TEN OUT OF TEN

IN terms of a 'great game for the neutral', you would be hard-pressed to find a better example than the Third Division (South) encounter between Argyle and Crystal Palace at snowy Selhurst Park on November 28th 1925. Argyle raced into a 4-1 half-time lead, with Jack Cock (2), Patsy Corcoran and Freddy Forbes having scored: 45 minutes later, they trailed 5-4 before Sammy Black equalised with the last kick of the game. The game entered the record books as Argyle's highest-scoring league draw.

FOUR FOUR-ALLS

FOUR 4-4 score draws have been witnessed at Home Park during the Greens' Football League lifetime. Sammy Black played and scored in the first two, both Second Division games, against West Ham United on August 30th 1933 – when Jimmy Cookson (2) and Tommy Grozier were also on the scoresheet – and Bradford City, on September 9th 1936, when Jack Vidler netted a couple and Fred Mitcheson also scored. After two 4-4s in three years, Home Park had to wait 34 seasons for another one. Sammy Black did not take part in the sharing with Shrewsbury Town of eight Third Division goals, six of which were scored by the Shrews: four for them and two own goals to add to the couple that Argyle players managed to score unassisted, through Don Hutchins and Dave Burnside. Interestingly, the goalkeepers in all four of the 4-4s were of high reputation: Bill Harper (against West Ham), Harry Cann (Bradford), Jim Furnell (Shrewsbury Town) and, in the latest of the high-scoring eight-goal encounters against Cardiff City on New Year's Day 1986, Geoff Crudgington; although Crudgie was only responsible for one of Cardiff's goals. He vacated his goal, after Garry Nelson's strike had restored parity at 1-1, because of a facial injury. Full-back Gordon Nisbet took over as goalkeeper, and let in three more opposition goals, but Kevin Summerfield, John Clayton and Kevin Hodges ensured honours were shared.

SHREWS HOLD OUT

ONLY one side prevented Argyle's 2001/02 Nationwide Third Division season from being an all-conquering one: Shrewsbury Town. The Shrews were the only side the Pilgrims failed to tame (sorry, could not avoid it), losing to them at both home – on the opening day of the season – and away.

CUP RUNNETH OVER

ARGYLE'S best performance in a cup competition – a situation in conjunction with which the words 'best' and 'performance' have rarely been used – came in January 1966, when the Second Division Pilgrims won a third-round FA Cup tie 6-0 at Home Park against… ahem, Corby Town. The Northamptonshire non-leaguers went out to a Mike Bickle hat-trick and goals from Norman Piper, Barrie Jones and Cliff Jackson. The Pilgrims have equalled that goalscoring record in a cup tournament on only two other occasions, once at home and once away. The away win came in 1906 when the Pilgrims were still a Southern League outfit and their FA Cup opponents were, again, non-league nonentities: New Crusaders. New Crusaders appear to be a family affair. Not only did their line-up include six brothers – Algernon, Archibald, Gilbert, Herbert, Percy and Bernard Farnfield – they also played on the grounds of Sidcup College, where their father was headmaster. They met Argyle in a qualifying round in their debut season and lost to a Harry Wilcox hat-trick and goals from Johnny Banks, Tommy Briercliffe and Percy Saul. The only time that Argyle have scored six goals against league opposition in the FA Cup came in a first-round tie on November 16th 1957, when they beat fellow Third Division (South) team Watford 6-2 at Home Park. Bernard Barnes and Wilf Carter both bagged braces, as they were fond of saying in that day, and Peter Anderson and Jimmy Gauld scored. Carter claimed a hat-trick in the following round, when the Pilgrims beat Dorchester 5-2 at home, before they bowed out of the competition 6-1 to Newcastle United at Home Park, which had witnessed 22 goals in three FA Cup games that season.

LONDON DOWN

WHILE the Pilgrims' 6-0 win over Corby is their highest winning margin in a cup competition, they have also lost cup matches twice by six goals. The first defeat was on January 19th 1910, when the Southern League Pilgrims lost 7-1 to Tottenham Hotspur in an FA Cup first-round replay, having bravely held the Londoners 1-1 at Home Park four days earlier. The second six-goal cup thrashing was also in the capital, more than half a decade later, when the Second Division Greens went down 6-0 to West Ham United in the Football League Cup on September 26th 1962.

PLYMOUTH ARGYLE NIL

THE Pilgrims' record for failing to score in consecutive league matches is a mind-numbing five games, a mark which has been 'achieved' on four occasions. The first time came at the end of the Second Division season of 1938/39, the last before the break caused by the Second World War. It began with a 0-0 shut-out at home to Chesterfield on March 11th 1939, and ended with a 1-0 defeat at Tottenham Hotspur on April 7th. In between, there had been a second consecutive goalless Home Park draw, against West Ham United, and defeat at Tranmere Rovers (0-2) and Bury (0-3). The barren spell was broken by a 1-1 home draw with Sheffield Wednesday. The second five-game goalless run came in the second Second Division season after cessation of hostilities. It began on September 20th 1947 with a 3-0 defeat at Cardiff City and ended on October 18th, with a 2-0 reverse by Tottenham at White Hart Lane. In between times, the Pilgrims had drawn 0-0 at home to Luton Town and at Brentford and lost 2-0 at home to Sheffield Wednesday. A 1-1 draw at home to Millwall saw the streak end. Three seasons later, a 2-0 defeat by Queens Park Rangers at Home Park on March 11th 1950 began another five-match sequence without a Green goal. A 0-0 draw at Preston North End followed before an away 3-0 loss at Coventry City was sandwiched between a 1-0 home defeat by Swansea and a goalless draw with Luton. A 2-1 home victory over Leicester City followed but it was a rare moment of joy in a disappointing Second Division season that saw the Pilgrims relegated. The writing had been on the wall since February 4th, when Argyle had warmed up for their record-equalling feat by notching up four games without a goal. Only a 2-2 draw at Grimsby Town on March 4th prevented the goalless sequence from being an incredible ten games. The fourth time the Pilgrims came away from five consecutive matches with no reward whatsoever was at the start of the 2005 Championship campaign. The second Saturday of the season saw a 2-0 home defeat by Derby County, after which followed successive 1-0 reverses, at Crystal Palace and at home to Hull, before a 2-0 Bank Holiday Monday loss at Brighton & Hove Albion cost manager Bobby Williamson his job. Number two Jocky Wilson finally reversed the trend with a 1-1 home draw against Crewe Alexandra, but not before he had overseen a 2-0 loss at Norwich City.

SCORING FOR FUN

AT the other end of the scale, the Pilgrims' record for scoring in consecutive league games runs for an impressive eight years. Okay, then, most of those years saw no league football because of the Second World War, but the streak either side of the hostilities does stretch to 39 consecutive matches in which they found the net at least once in every game. The sequence began at Swansea Town on April 15th 1939 with a 2-1 Second Division defeat in the Principality in which Ernie Smith netted the Greens' consolation. Thirty-nine games later, on April 12th 1947, a 1-0 loss to Newcastle at Home Park brought to an end the Pilgrims' goalfest. In 26 of the matches, someone called 'Thomas' had scored; either Dave or his brother Bob (or, more occasionally than you might have thought, both). Dave, who played for the Pilgrims both before and after the war, found the net 22 times, while Bob, who played only in the one post-war campaign, claimed 12 strikes in the streak. Other notable contributors included Sid Rawlings (17) and Billy Strauss (eight), while there were also three own goals.

BORN TO IT

PERHAPS the two most appropriate players to represent Argyle were C. Green (three appearances, one goal, 1910), and Mike Green (122 appearances, ten goals, 1974-77).

HOME OR AWAY

IT tells you all you need to know about the Pilgrims' erratic behaviour immediately following the Second World War that part of the club record 39 consecutive games in which they did not fail to find the net also coincides with a 31-game streak in which they did not draw a match – another club record. The Win, Lose But No Draw sequence began almost exactly halfway into the Score Every Game Run, after Burnley had come away from Home Park with a point from a 2-2 deadlock. Following that, Argyle either won or lost every league game they played in until four games into the 1947-48 campaign. I say won or lost, but the last nine matches of the streak were lost – another club record. Plymouth city centre stores allegedly ran out of anoraks as Home Park became a heaven for stattos in the immediate post-war era.

LOTS OF LITTLEWOODS

ARGYLE'S 6-3 FA Cup defeat of New Crusaders at the beginning of the 20th century is the highest scoring cup match in which the Pilgrims have participated. However, they have equalled a share of nine goals twice in League Cup matches – that's matches, not ties. In 1986, the Third Division Greens lost a Littlewoods Challenge Cup game 5-4 at Cardiff in the first leg of a first-round tie at Ninian Park, where former Bluebird Kevin Summerfield was on the scoresheet, alongside Gordon Nisbet and two-goal Russell Coughlin. Despite the advantage of four away goals, the Pilgrims went out of the same competition 6-4 on aggregate after losing the resumption the following week, 1-0. Two seasons later, the now Second Division Pilgrims failed to build on a similarly decent position when, after losing only 1-0 away in the first leg of a second-round tie against Manchester City, they were soundly beaten in the return, 6-3. Mark Smith, Sean McCarthy and Tommy Tynan scored the Argyle goals.

DOUBLE FIGURES

ARGYLE have only once scored 10 goals in a game – when they defeated Bristol City in the 1939/40 South West Regional League, introduced to replace the Football League divisions after the outbreak of the Second World War. Jackie Smith scored four times, Leonard Townsend netted a hat-trick, William McDonald notched twice, and Bill Olver scored.

DIRTY SHEETS

BETWEEN Boxing Day 1962-September 1963, the Pilgrims played 24 Second Division matches. In none of them did they keep a clean sheet. The sequence began with a 4-2 home victory over Cardiff City and did not end until a rather unlikely 0-0 draw at Preston North End on September 9th 1963. During the two dozen games, Argyle conceded 59 goals, an average of around two and half goals a game, and scored 42. There were some fairly notable results along the way – a 5-4 home defeat by Middlesbrough, and a 5-0 away loss to the same opponents; a 3-1 home win over Leeds United in which Peter McParland scored a hat-trick; a 6-3 defeat by Charlton Athletic at the Valley; and a 4-3 home loss to Newcastle United. The goalkeeping duties during the run were shared by Dave MacLaren and John Leiper.

WELCOME TO HOME PARK

THE record for home games without a clean sheet is 15 matches, a streak which has been achieved twice. The first spanned the 1930/31 and 1931/32 Second Division seasons and began with a 3-1 win against Reading on April 18th 1931. The next time Home Park witnessed a shut-out was on February 13th 1932, when Barnsley failed to trouble the scorers. In the run, Argyle conceded 26 goals, including four against Notts County and three against Bristol City, and scored 51, eight of which came in the club record victory over Millwall. Nottingham Forest and Bury were both dispatched 5-1.

OPEN GOAL

THE second 15-match league streak in which Argyle failed to keep a clean sheet at Home Park spanned the 1967/68 Second Division relegation season and the start of the subsequent 1968/69 campaign. It started with a 1-0 home defeat by Queens Park Rangers on Boxing Day 1967 and did not end until Mike Bickle's goal gave the Pilgrims a 1-0 victory over Walsall the following September. Argyle conceded 24 goals in the 15 games, only five of which they won, including successive 3-1s against Reading and Bristol immediately before unsaddling themselves of a new record with victory over Walsall.

NOUGHTIE FORTIES

ARGYLE have twice put together five-match home sequences in which they have failed to score a league goal, within four post-Second World War seasons of each other. The first time covered the end of the 1946/47 campaign and the beginning of the 1947/48 one. Between April 12th, when Newcastle won 1-0 and September 3rd, when Leicester shared the spoils in a 0-0 draw, Argyle lost twice in three matches to Birmingham City (2-0 in 1946/47, and 3-0 in 1947/48) and 2-0 to Millwall before beating Barnsley 1-0 to break a run that was repeated towards the end of the 1949/50 season. Then, the rot set in with a 0-0 draw against Blackburn Rovers on February 18th and continued with successive defeats by Sheffield United (1-0), Queens Park Rangers (2-0) and Swansea Town (1-0) before another goalless encounter, with Luton Town. The sequence-busters in this case were Leicester City, against whom the Pilgrims not only scored, through Billy Strauss and George Dews, but also won, 2-1.

A WINTER'S TALE

THE winter of 1989/90 was a long and cheerless one for Pilgrims fans, who did not see a Second Division home win at Home Park for more than three months; the eight-game lose-and-draw streak at home being Argyle's worst in front of their own fans. The run began on October 28th 1989 when Blackburn Rovers held Ken Brown's men 2-2, Sean McCarthy netting twice for the Greens. There followed draws against Bradford City (1-1), West Bromwich Albion (2-2) and West Ham United (1-1) and defeats by Port Vale (2-1), Portsmouth (2-0), Hull City (2-1) and Wolverhampton Wanderers (1-0) before the Pilgrims spectacularly bust the jinx with a fine 3-0 victory over Sunderland, Tommy Tynan scoring twice.

CAN'T WIN

NOT surprisingly, Argyle's all-time losing streak also makes a major contribution to their record Home Park sequence of losses, which spans the 1946/47 and 1947/48 seasons. As if life in post-Second World War Plymouth was not bleak enough. The run began with spirited defeats by Tottenham Hotspur (4-3, on March 29th 1947) and Bradford Park Avenue (4-2) before Newcastle United, Birmingham City (twice, once in either season) and Millwall came and went with maximum returns and without conceding. The 0-0 home draw against Leicester City on September 3rd 1948 again proved to be a streak-buster.

FORTRESS HOME PARK

THE Pilgrims' record for consecutive league home wins and consecutive games at Home Park without a draw is one and the same. It will not come as a shock that the 17-match Third Division (South) run comes from the 47-game spell in which they did not suffer a home defeat. It began on the final day of 1921, when Swansea Town were defeated 3-1 and was maintained for the remaining ten matches of the 1921/22 season, the last five of which saw goalkeeper Fred Craig keep a clean sheet while his forwards banged in 14 goals. The sequence was kept up for the opening seven home games of the 1922/23 campaign, which began with a rather pleasing 5-1 victory over Bristol City, before, on November 25th 1923, Southend United held out for a 1-1 draw.

KEN BROWN: WINTER OF DISCONTENT

CAN'T SCORE

ARGYLE'S record for consecutive clean sheets in home matches came in only their second season in the Football League, and first in the Third Division (South), 1921/22. The ten-game Home Park run in which no opponents scored began on September 3rd 1921, when Bert Bowler gave the Pilgrims a 1-0 home win over Bristol Rovers. Five more victories followed (against Gillingham, 3-0; Luton Town, 2-0; Reading, 2-0; Newport County, 1-0; and Swindon Town, 1-0) in which Frank Richardson was on target in every game, before successive 0-0s against Merthyr Town and Portsmouth. A 4-0 win over Southend United followed before Exeter City settled for a 0-0 on December 27th. Argyle finally conceded a home goal on the final day of the year when Swansea Town offset a 3-1 beating by finally scoring an opposition goal at Home Park. Coincidence or not, it was the first game of the run in which Fred Craig had not kept goal, Bill Cook deputising.

GOALS GALORE

HOME Park was the place to be in the mid-1920s if you wanted to see goals – especially Argyle goals. For nearly two years, spanning three Third Division (South) seasons, the Pilgrims did not fail to score in a home game. The 39-match streak in which they found the net at least once in a home league match began with an inauspicious 1-0 victory over Watford, courtesy of a Sammy Black goal, on March 14th 1925. The Pilgrims netted at home in the subsequent six matches of the 1924/25 campaign, and throughout the entire following 1925/26 season. They extended the sequence to more than halfway through the next 1926/27 season right up until January 29th 1927, when, after 120 goals (an average of more than three per game) Gillingham parked the charabanc in front of their goal and stodged out a 0-0 draw. Some highlights of the extraordinary streak included; three successive home games in which Argyle scored six goals, two of which were against the same opponents, Southend United (6-0 in the last game of the 1924/25 season, and 6-2 in the first game of the 1925/26 season) and another against Crystal Palace; seven goals against Bristol City, Aberdare Athletic and Bournemouth & Boscombe Athletic; and four goals in a game for Jack Cock against Norwich City. In fact, Cock scored 37 of the 120 goals in the sequence, and he was supported by Jack Leslie (22), Freddy Forbes (18), and Sammy Black (14).

DRAW YOUR OWN CONCLUSIONS

THE club record for consecutive home league draws is an unremarkable four games – a mark which has been hit on four occasions. The first time it happened was in 1953, when the Pilgrims drew the opening four games of their Second Division season, beginning with a 1-1 stalemate against Bury on August 19th, following that with 2-2s against Birmingham and Luton (in which the goalscorers – Eric Davis and Maurice Tadman – were identical), before another 1-1 against Leeds. The sequence was broken by Rotherham United, who won 2-0 on September 19th. Nearly 40 years passed before the run was replicated, this time over two Barclays Second Division seasons, the last two games of the 1989/90 season and the first two of the 1990/91 campaign. The four-game progression began on April 21th with a 1-1 draw against Newcastle United and continued a week later with a 0-0 season-ending draw against Watford. The Hornets were also the first visitors to Home Park of the 1990/91 season, and drew 1-1. Another 1-1 followed, against Middlesbrough before, on September 15th, the Pilgrims beat Leicester 2-0. Two seasons later, around Christmas time, Peter Shilton's Pilgrims matched the four-match home-draw run. Hartlepool were the first of a quartet of Barclay's Second Division sides to claim a share of the points in a 2-2 draw on December 12th, while Home Park's festive match proved to be a bit of a turkey, the encounter with West Bromwich Albion ending goalless. Home Park had to wait nearly a month for its next action, which turned out to be a 1-1 draw with Fulham, before another goalless game, against Hull. It was not until February 6th 1993 that the home crowd finally had a victory to cheer, when Kevin Nugent scored a hat-trick in a 3-2 win over Mansfield. The start to the Pilgrims' most successful season for more than half a century in 2007/08 also saw four consecutive home deadlocks. Ian Holloway's Championship side opened their home campaign on August 18th with a 1-1 draw against Ipswich Town before a goalless stalemate with Leicester. A fortnight later, two goals from Sylvan Ebanks-Blake against Cardiff made it a hat-trick of home draws, and, two weeks later, Nick Chadwick salvaged a point in a 1-1 divvy-up with Wolves. The home fans eventually celebrated a victory on October 2nd, when a goal from Péter Halmosi gave the Pilgrims a 1-0 triumph over Crystal Palace. Despite the stuttering start, in which eight points were effectively dropped, Argyle finished the campaign in tenth place – six points outside the end-of-season play-off positions.

RUNNING AWAY WITH IT

THE Pilgrims' record for consecutive away league wins – six – was achieved over two Third Division (South) seasons, 1928/29 and 1929/30, at the end of which they won promotion to the Second Division. The run began with the final away game of the 1928/29 season, on April 27th, when two goals from Jack Leslie finished off the campaign with a 2-0 win at Brentford. A second successive 2-0 win in London followed on the first day of the 1929/30 season, August 31st, when Ray Bowden and Sammy Black accounted for Clapton Orient. Two Westcountry away wins followed, at Torquay (4-3) and Bristol Rovers (3-2) before it was back up country for another 2-0 away win, this time at Watford. The final game of the run came at Swindon Town, 2-1, before the Pilgrims' travels finally caught up with them at Northampton Town on October 19th, when they were held to a 1-1 draw.

SHUT OUT

ARGYLE have twice enjoyed a run of four league games in which they did not concede a goal. The first time came in their very first season as a Football League club, in the Third Division. Effective they might have been from Home Park, they could hardly be accused of being a joy to watch. Three 0-0 draws on the spin, from September 1st to the 18th 1920 against Crystal Palace, Norwich City and Newport County, were followed by a single goal victory at Gillingham, on October 2nd, courtesy of Ginger Hill. The sequence was broken a fortnight later, when Swindon Town netted in a 1-1 draw.

TIGHT LINES

ARGYLE'S first ever campaign as a Football League club was as tight as they come. Not only did they achieve a club record four consecutive shut-outs in league games away from Home Park, they also set another best sequence which has never been beaten – four consecutive draws on the road. The streak, either side of Christmas, began with (another) 0-0 at Merthyr Town on December 18th 1920 and was followed by three successive 1-1s between December 27th and February 5th, at Exeter City, where Moses Russell scored; Grimsby Town, with Ginger Hill netting; and Portsmouth, where William Toms notched. The run came to an end on March 5th, when Swansea Town beat the Pilgrims 3-0.

HIT FOR SIX

THE Pilgrims' record for failing to score in successive away matches stands at six matches – a sequence which has been reached six times. The first time they drew a blank in six consecutive games on the road was over the Christmas and New Year period of the 1922/23 Third Division (South) season. The run began at Watford (1-0) on December 16th 1922, took in Northampton Town (0-1), Brentford (0-2), Norwich City (0-1), Gillingham (0-1) and Brighton & Hove Albion (…you've guessed, 0-1). Six defeats, but only seven goals conceded. A 3-2 victory at Queens Park Rangers on March 15th ended a three-month barren away spell in style, John Devine (2) and Jack Fowler scoring. It was nearly 45 years later that the Pilgrims matched the sorry sequence, the early days of the 1967/68 relegation season. Between September 2nd and October 28th, they conceded 17 goals, including 5-0s at Crystal Palace and Middlesbrough, before a 1-1 draw at Ipswich Town on November 25th, thanks to John Mitten's strike, saw them finally score. David Kemp's 1990/91 and 1991/92 Barclays Second Division teams matched the Pilgrims' six-away-games-without-a-win worst. The streak began on March 30th 1991 with a 1-0 reverse at Barnsley, and continued until the end of the season, with a 2-0 defeat at Hull City. In between, the Greens had visited Bristol Rovers (0-0) and Oxford United (0-0) as well as Notts County, where a side managed by future Argyle boss Neil Warnock won 4-0, thanks to a hat-trick from future Pilgrim Dave Regis. The road-trip difficulties hung over until the following 1991/92 campaign, where an opening-day 2-0 loss at Leicester City set the tone for a relegation season. Although a new away-worst was staved off by a 2-2 draw at, of all places, Newcastle United, the six-game streak was repeated towards the end of the season. There are three things noteworthy of the sequence, the first of which was that it was presided over by four different managers. Watford's 1-0 win on February 8th was Kemp's last away match as manager, with caretaker bosses Gordon Nisbet and Alan Gillett subsequently taking care of the team at Ipswich Town (0-2). Peter Shilton was in charge of the latter two-thirds of the run at Wolverhampton Wanderers (0-1), former club Derby County (0-2), Port Vale (0-1) and Charlton Athletic. Noteworthy point number two was that the Charlton match, which was played at Upton Park, was Shilton's playing debut for the Pilgrims. The third noteworthy point was that the run was broken by a Dwight Marshall inspired 1-0 win at that year's FA Cup finalists Sunderland on April 16th – a Thursday – and was the only time that the Pilgrims won at Roker Park.

A QUESTION OF PERSPECTIVE

THE last two times Argyle have failed to score in a record-equalling six successive away matches came in the 21st century. Staying in the Championship was the Pilgrims' motivation in the 2005/06 season, and they achieved this comfortably under Tony Pulis's austere style which saw a six-game scoreless away spell in which Argyle nevertheless picked up three points and conceded only three goals. Between February 4th and April 8th, they lost at Burnley (0-1), drew at Stoke City (0-0), lost at Derby County and Hull City (both 0-1) and drew at Preston North End and Leeds United (both 0-0). The run was broken at Millwall, where a goal from Vincent Péricard secured a 1-1 draw. The final instance of a six-game away run without a goal came in the 2008/09 Championship season, as the Pilgrims went from play-off contenders to relegation candidates between November 25th and January 31st. Every match was a tight one, but Argyle took only two points from 0-0 draws against Southampton and Ipswich Town that sandwiched defeats at Doncaster Rovers (0-1), Barnsley (0-2), Cardiff City (0-1) and Nottingham Forest (0-1). A 1-1 draw at Preston North End, where Jamie Mackie scored, meant an unwanted seventh game was avoided.

CASHING IN

MALCOLM Allison was paid a salary of £3,000 per annum when he joined the Pilgrims as manager in May 1964.

ABSOLUTELY FABULOUS

WITH a forward line including the likes of Jack Cock, Sammy Black, Jack Leslie and Freddy Forbes, goals were barely a problem for Argyle in their first decade. The fab four were well on target during the 1926/27 and 1927/28 Third Division (South) seasons, when the Pilgrims set a club record away scoring sequence of 22 consecutive matches without failing to notch. The sequence began with a 2-1 win at Brighton & Hove Albion in December 1926 and ended a day shy of a calendar year later with a 2-0 win at Brentford, before a 2-0 defeat at Millwall snapped the streak. Argyle scored 46 goals in the 22 games, the highlight of which was probably a 6-5 victory at Aberdare Athletic on January 22nd 1927, which came three weeks after a 6-2 New Year's Day defeat at Bournemouth & Boscombe Athletic.

HOLES ON THE ROAD

EVEN the longest-suffering Argyle fan will be amazed to hear that the Pilgrims once went nearly eight years without keeping a clean sheet in a league game away from Home Park. That is not being terribly fair, as, for six of those years football was lost to the Second World War. Nevertheless, the Pilgrims still went the best part of the equivalent of two whole seasons, including the whole of the 1946/47 Second Division campaign, without keeping a single clean sheet away from Home Park in 42 games. The run began at Bradford Park Avenue on October 22nd 1938, when Harry Lane and Charlie Fletcher scored in a 2-2 draw. By the end of the Second Division season, the Pilgrims had failed to win any of their remaining 15 matches, losing ten and drawing five. The following season, all 21 Argyle away matches saw at least one opposition goal as the Pilgrims lost 16, won three and drew two matches on their travels – lowlights included a 6-1 stuffing at Birmingham, and 5-1 losses at Southampton and Nottingham Forest, while West Bromwich Albion were beaten 5-2 and Luton 4-3. The Pilgrims stayed up, though, and approached the new season with confidence which turned out to be wildly misplaced as the away campaign kicked off with a 6-1 loss at Newcastle. After another loss at Leicester City (2-1) and a draw at West Bromwich Albion (1-1), back-to-back losses at Leeds United (5-0) and Cardiff City (3-0) followed before the rot was stopped with a 0-0 draw at Luton Town.

WHOSE SIDE ARE YOU ON, REF?

BARROW celebrated a new club record of 18 Third Division home games without defeat thanks to a home win against Argyle on November 9th 1968, and thanks to referee Ivan Robinson, who 'scored' the only goal of the game. Robinson, standing just inside the penalty area, accidently got in the way of a shot from outside the box by Barrow's George McLean. The ball hit the inside of his left foot and deflected off at a peculiar angle, with Argyle goalkeeper Pat Dunne, who had moved to cover the shot, being left stranded when the ball went the other way. Not one Argyle player protested – they just stood and stared in sheer amazement. To make matters worse, MacLean was a former Exeter City player.

COUPON-BUSTERS

ARGYLE'S popularity with pools punters dipped considerably in the mid-1950s when, for more than a year, they failed to register a draw away from Home Park. Between October 16th 1954 and November 19th 1955, Argyle played 26 Second Division matches and failed to share the points once. After starting out with a club record nine successive away defeats, they managed to win on the road only four times in the subsequent 16 matches, losing a total of 22 of the 26 games away from home. The match that broke the 13-month win-or-lose sequence came on December 3rd 1955, when the Pilgrims drew 0-0 at Rotherham United. They were relegated to the Third Division (South) at the end of the season.

REAL DEAL

THE undoubted highlight of Argyle's pre-season visit to Austria in 2006 – in fact, the highlight of any Argyle pre-season – was a prestige friendly against Fabio Capello's Real Madrid. We can only wonder what Capello made of then-boss Ian Holloway, who quite literally threw himself off his chair when asked what his reaction was to being given such a high-profile game in his first weeks as Pilgrims' manager. Argyle lost, but only to a second-half penalty by Brazilian Julio Baptista, one of eight full internationals in the Spaniards' starting line-up. Argyle had two – Norwegian-born Northern Irishman Tony Capaldi and London-born Jamaican Barry Hayles. The penalty was awarded after Argyle's French midfielder Lilian Nalis handled in the area.

Argyle (4-4-2) first half : Luke McCormick; Anthony Barness, Mathias Kouo-Doumbe, Hasney Aljofree, Gary Sawyer; David Norris, Luke Summerfield, Lee Hodges, Ryan Dickson; Chris Zebroski, Barry Hayles. Second half: Josh Clapham; Paul Connolly, Mauro Almeida, Scott Laird, Tony Capaldi; Reuben Reid, Lilian Nalis, Paul Wotton, Bojan Djordjic; Nick Chadwick, Sylvan Ebanks-Blake. Real Madrid (4-2-3-1): Diego Lopez; Carlos Diogo, Ivan Helguera, Jonathan Woodgate, Raul Bravo; Guti, Thomas Gravesen; Juanfran, Julio Baptista, Antonio Cassano; Javier Portillo.

TONY CAPALDI: REAL THING

DRAW SOME COMFORT

THE two occasions other than Argyle's debut Football League campaign when the Pilgrims have achieved four successive draws came three decades after the first, and then three decades after that. Surprisingly, the side that was relegated from the Second Division in 1949/50 put together a decent springtime run that saw them take a share of the spoils in successive games from February 4th to March 18th 1950. The run began at Brentford on February 4th, with a goalless game at Brentford, a scoreline matched at Leicester City the following week. On March 4th, two goals from George Dews secured a 2-2 draw at Grimsby Town, and, a fortnight later, it was stalemate again with another 0-0 at Preston North End. The run was broken at Coventry on April 1st, when the Pilgrims felt a little more than foolish after losing 3-0. The Pilgrims' first four games of the 1980/81 Third Division campaign also ended as draws. They kicked off the campaign at Colchester United, where David Kemp and Donal Murphy secured the better half of a 2-2 draw, and followed that with a goalless stalemate at Oxford United a fortnight later. Two further weeks passed before another 2-2, at Chesterfield, where David Kemp was again on the mark along with Mark Graves, followed by a 1-1 in a midweek match at Reading, Murphy again notching. Another David Kemp goal, and one from John Sims, brought the run to an end with a 2-0 win at Newport County.

ON THE BUTTON

YOU probably do not even need to know any match details to realise that Argyle's 0-0 Third Division draw against Bristol Rovers in February 1992 in front of less than 7,000 supporters was pretty dire fare. Half-time, though, was a different matter altogether. A young fan at the Barn Park end of Home Park brightened the atmosphere by sending a remote-controlled car from his position in the terracing out across the pitch. He made it run up and down a few times, and spun it around – showing greater dexterity than those he had been watching for 45 minutes – and then positioned it on the penalty spot. Using his controls, he sent it careering into the goal to a mighty cheer from the crowd. The car then wheeled full circle, as if accepting the applause, before returning to its master.

SEASIDE SPECIAL

A 2-0 victory at Blackpool is not generally regarded as something to get too excited about, but when Argyle snuck away from Bloomfield Road with a Second Division win on October 9th 1976, thanks to goals from Doug Collins and Micky Horswill, there was a rare feeling of triumph. 'Rare' being the operative word. For it had been two seasons previously that they had managed to collect full points on the road. Following a 2-0 win at Huddersfield Town on April 8th 1975, the Pilgrims went 27 winless games before they tasted another league win on their trips from Home Park. It started with a 0-0 draw at Walsall, after which Tony Waiters' men beat Colchester United 1-0 at Home Park to gain promotion from the Third Division, and the 1974/75 season petered out with a 1-1 draw at Grimsby Town and a 1-0 defeat at Peterborough United. It took the Pilgrims four games in the higher echelon to register a first point, in a 1-1 draw at Luton, and that was about as good as it got during the entire campaign. They drew a further seven games and lost 13 in total as they went through the entire season without an away victory. None. Not one. Nil, Zip, Zero. Nada. The high point of their travels was probably a 2-2 draw against Bristol City at Ashton Gate. However, although they secured only eight points out of 42 away from Home Park, they amassed 30 at home – the fourth-best home record in the division – to finish far from trouble. The 1976/77 season, which ended in relegation, began with two 2-2 draws, at Oldham Athletic and Orient, and a 3-0 loss at Millwall before that happy trip to the Seasiders.

BOWLING ALONG

ARGYLE won the Devon Professional Championship 23 times between the 1922/23 season, when it was inaugurated, and 1995, after which it became the Devon St. Luke's Bowl. Originally contested for between Argyle, Exeter City and Torquay United, the Pilgrims dominated the tournament in its early days but the rise of the modern game saw the competition undergo changes to include local non-league sides and, from the early part of the current century, the Pilgrims' youth side has contested on behalf of Argyle. In 1960, Argyle played a joint Exeter-Torquay side and, in 1993 and 1994, after some time off the calendar, it was played for as a pre-season tournament.

CAVE TRAGEDY

MICKY Cave, who scored four goals in eight Third Division games for the Pilgrims at the end of the 1971/72 season, was another Pilgrim who met an untimely end. Cave later emigrated to America and became assistant coach of Major Indoor Soccer League team Pittsburgh Spirit, but died at the age of 35 from carbon monoxide poisoning. According to the *New York Times*, "police said Cave's car was found in the basement garage of his condominium with the ignition on, the engine cold and the gas tank empty. Detectives said there was no suicide note and that Cave had been in good health".

TURNING-POINT

ARGYLE'S record for consecutive away games without defeat (12) came in one of the most successful seasons, the 2001/02 Third Division campaign in which they dominated the division and would have run away with the title if it had not been for Luton Town. The season, though, didn't start well and, by the time the Pilgrims visited Rushden & Diamonds on August Bank Holiday Monday 27th, they had just one point from their opening three games. After 40 minutes at Nene Park, they were 2-0 down to a pair of Duane Darby goals. Just before half-time, a Michael Evans goal reduced the deficit, and Graham Coughlan equalised in the second half. The comeback seemed all for nowt, though, when Rushden defender Mark Peters powered a free header towards the Argyle goal. However, goalkeeper Romain Larrieu made a spectacular season-turning save to keep the scores level, and Brian McGlinchey grabbed a winner. The Pilgrims added another ten games to their unbeaten away streak, including a satisfying 3-2 victory at Exeter City, before tasting defeat on their travels three days before Christmas Day, 2-1 at Scunthorpe United. They suffered just three more away losses all season, however – at Luton Town, Shrewsbury Town, and Hartlepool United – as they ran off with the title.

200 CLUB

BETWEEN 1921 and 1927, when Argyle were runners-up for six consecutive Third Division seasons, they played 252 matches, won 143 and drew 55. Consistency was the keyword in the 1920s, with goalkeeper Fred Craig, Moses Russell, Jack Leslie, Jimmy Logan and Sammy Black racking up 200-plus appearances.

HARDIE ANNUAL

ALEC Hardie was rewarded for his 241 appearances for the Pilgrims between 1926-33 with a Benefit Match that no doubt sweetened the bitter pill of having to join Exeter City. Alec's Benefit was between the Pilgrims and Partick Thistle in April 1933, and, although Argyle lost 3-2, there was more to this game which affected Argyle's future. Greens' manager Robert Jack was impressed with two Partick players and offered them the chance to sign for Argyle. One, John Simpson, played only five matches before having to quit the game through injury. The other, Jimmy Rae, played 283 times for the Pilgrims before becoming Argyle manager and eventually leading them to the Third Division (South) title in 1951-52.

WHAT A GUY

BARRIE Vassallo was the only player to reach the top three in the Goal of the Month competition on *Match of the Day* when the programme ruled the airwaves – he came third for his goal against Everton in the FA Cup fourth-round match on January 25th 1975. Barrie was making his first starting appearance for Argyle, having played twice before as substitute, and was a surprise inclusion in the team for Paul Mariner whose injury had been hushed up. His second claim to fame was that he had a song written about him by local musician Dave Banana (probably not his real name). Vassallo was difficult to fit into the very clever lyrics of I Saw Them Play, which name-checks the players in several of Argyle's more famous teams, so Dave came up with the tribute tune Barrie Vassallo – What A Guy as an extra hidden track on an Argyle-themed CD. Barrie, one of only four Argyle players whose surname has begun with the letter V, scored twice more in a total of 15 appearances for the Greens, and finished his Football League career at Torquay where, in his final game, he was a substitute for future Argyle chief scout Lindsay Parsons.

PENALTY TREBLE

AN Argyle player once scored a hat-trick of penalties. Tony McShane netted all three of the Pilgrims' goals in a reserve game at Home Park against Portsmouth on August 27th 1952. Argyle won the match 3-1. Portsmouth scored from open play.

BUS TOP

ARGYLE were a driven team when they visited Bournemouth in the 1974/75 Third Division promotion season, coming away from Dean Court with a 7-3 victory, the second-highest total they have ever scored away from Home Park. Goals from Billy Rafferty, Paul Mariner (2), Brian Johnson, Hughie McAuley, John Delve and Colin Randell kept the promotion bandwagon on track, but the real secret of the Pilgrims' success was that they travelled along the coast in a brand new £25,000 first-team coach.

PLYMOUTH UNITED

AFTER crowd trouble in France during the first leg of the 1977/78 Cup-Winners' Cup first-round tie between Manchester United and AS Saint-Étienne, United were fined £7,500 and ordered to play the second leg at least 300 kilometres away from Old Trafford. They plumped for Home Park, and won the match 2-0 in front of a crowd of 31,634. The United team was: Alex Stepney, Jimmy Nicholl, Arthur Albiston, Sammy McIlroy, Brian Greenhoff, Martin Buchan, Steve Coppell, Jimmy Greenhoff, Stuart Pearson, Lou Macari and Gordon Hill. Coppell and Pearson scored the goals.

SAW POINT

DEFENDER Chris Barker nearly missed his Argyle debut on the opening day of the 2008/09 Championship season because of a family heirloom. Chris took part in the Pilgrims' 2-2 draw at home to Wolverhampton Wanderers on August 9th after team-mates Jason Puncheon and Steve MacLean took drastic action to remove a ring from his finger… with a hacksaw. As Chris was walking out of the changing-room, the referee told him he was not allowed to wear any rings and that he would have to remove one that his father gave him before he passed away. He achieved it with seconds to spare and a cut finger. The club later paid for the ring to be repaired.

KEEPING ON

ENGLAND and Everton keeper Ted Sagar's second appearance at Home Park came in a Second Division match on 15 November 1952… more than 21 years after his first, in a 2-0 FA Cup defeat on January 10th 1931.

QUICK ON THE TRIGGER

MICHAEL Evans gave life to his dressing-room nickname 'Trigger', when some quick thinking helped give the Pilgrims a 2-1 victory over Second Division promotion rivals Swindon Town at Home Park on March 13th 2004. Evans brought to an end Swindon's unbeaten run at 11 games and maintained the Pilgrims' five-point lead at the top of the table when Argyle were awarded an indirect free-kick in the penalty area in the final ten minutes. Evans immediately tried to play a pass off his namesake in the Swindon goal, Rhys Evans, but the Swindon keeper made a grab at the ball as it went past him and conceded an own goal. The strike proved invaluable as Argyle, who had led from the 11th minute through Marino Keith's opportunist opener, conceded a late header to Tommy Mooney.

JUST A FEW

BETWEEN the ten seasons from 1920 to 1930, the Argyle defence conceded fewer goals than any other club in league football. Their full record was: played 420, won 227, drew 110, lost 90; goals for 774, goals against 430.

FANS FOR THE MEMORIES

PLYMOUTH Argyle Supporters Club was founded on January 22nd 1925. Archie Cload was first chairman. He later became a director.

POST OP

ARGYLE'S League Cup tie at Chester in 1981 was called off with the scores level. And the goal levelled. With the scores of the first-round tie level on September 2nd at 2-2, Pilgrims' striker David Kemp let fly with a shot that home goalkeeper Grenville Millington dived to save. He went crashing into the goalpost, which snapped just above ground level, leaving a short stub. The remainder was set in two feet of concrete and attempts to effect a repair were fruitless, so the match was abandoned, thus giving rise to a rare occasion of a two-leg cup-tie needing a replay after the first leg. That, too, ended all square at 1-1, Argyle's goal having been generously contributed by home defender Trevor Storton, and the Pilgrims won the second leg at Home Park 1-0, with local winger Tony Dennis scoring his only Greens goal.

SCROOBY DO

THE Pilgrims were English separatists who, in the first years of the 17th century, broke away from the Church of England because they felt that it had not completed the work of the Reformation and committed themselves to a life based on the Bible. One of the separatist congregations was led by William Brewster and the Rev Richard Clifton in the village of Scrooby in Nottinghamshire. The Scrooby group emigrated to Amsterdam in 1608 to escape harassment and religious persecution, and then moved to Leiden, where, enjoying full religious freedom, they remained for almost 12 years. In 1617, discouraged by economic difficulties, the pervasive Dutch influence on their children, and their inability to secure civil autonomy, the congregation voted to emigrate to America. A small ship, the *Speedwell*, carried them to Southampton, England, where they were to join another group of separatists and pick up a second ship. After some delays and disputes, the voyagers regrouped at Plymouth aboard the 180-ton *Mayflower*. It began its historic voyage on September 6th, 1620, with about 102 passengers on board, and, after a 65-day journey, the Pilgrims sighted Cape Cod on November 19th. Because they had no legal right to settle in the region, they drew up the Mayflower Compact, creating their own government. The settlers soon discovered Plymouth Harbour, on the western side of Cape Cod Bay and made their historic landing on December 21st; the main body of settlers followed on December 26th. The term 'Pilgrim' was first used by William Bradford to describe the Leiden Separatists who were leaving Holland. The Mayflower's passengers were first described as the Pilgrim Fathers in 1799. History was never this fun at school.

ONE FOR ME...

TERRY Austin had a pretty decent strike-rate in his 69 games for Argyle between 1976 and 1978, netting 20 goals. No match in which he netted was odder than the 2-2 Third Division draw against Lincoln City at Sincil Bank on January 2nd 1978. Terry opened the scoring after nine minutes, only to equalise his own strike with an oggie nine minutes later. Not to be outdone, Lincoln's Phil Neale, the former Worcestershire cricket captain, then amazingly matched Austin's achievement with a goal for each side, for Lincoln in 26 minutes and for Argyle in 44.

CARROW FELLOWS

ARGYLE have won promotion only eight times in their history. The first time was in 1929/30, when they climbed from the Third Division (South) to the Second with the crucial points being picked up in a 2-1 victory at Norwich City on April 28th. Manager Bob Jack's Pilgrims line-up at Carrow Road was: Harry Cann, Harry Bland, Frank Sloan, Walter Price, Jack Leslie, Jack Vidler, Tommy Grozier, Fred McKenzie, Billy Fellowes, Sammy Black, William Pullen.

BRIGHT BOYS

THE Pilgrims' second ever promotion, in 1951/52, was, like the first, from the Third Division (South) to the Second Division, and, like the first, it was secured away from home, this time at Brighton & Hove Albion. A 3-2 win for Jimmy Rae's side on April 23rd 1952, ensured they escaped the third tier at the second attempt after relegation in 1950, with George Dews, Alex Govan and Gordon Astall netting in front of a Goldstone Ground crowd of 28,000. The winning team was: Bill Shortt, Paddy Ratcliffe, Pat Jones, Tony McShane, Jumbo Chisholm, Alex Govan, Gordon Astall, George Dews, Maurice Tadman, Johnny Porteous, Peter Rattray.

HOMING IN ON TITLE

A THIRD successive win in April achieved Argyle's third successive title – and promotion to the Second Division in 1958/59 – after three years in the Third Division (South). It was the first time that the Pilgrims had gone up in front of their own fans – nearly 27,000 of them – and Jack Rowley's men achieved it with a 1-1 draw on April 29th, 1959, Wilf Carter netting in the stalemate with Bradford City. Argyle: Geoff Barnsley, George Robertson, Harry Penk, Johnny Williams, Gordon Fincham, Len Casey, Reg Wyatt, Jimmy Gauld, Peter Anderson, Wilf Carter, John 'Cardiff' Williams.

COMPASS DOUBLE

ARGYLE are the most westerly and the most southerly English league team in the country.

APRIL COOL

FOR the second time in three promotion seasons, April 29th was a red-letter day for the Greens. On that day in 1986, 20,000 people (and the rest) crammed into Home Park to see Dave Smith's team notch a 4-0 Third Division victory over Bristol City, goals courtesy of Tommy Tynan (2), Garry Nelson and Russell Coughlin, and promotion to the 1986/87 Today Second Division. Argyle: Geoff Crudgington, Gordon Nisbet, Leigh Cooper, Kevin Summerfield, Clive Goodyear, Tommy Tynan, Kevin Hodges, Russell Coughlin, John Matthews, Gerry McElhinney, Garry Nelson.

PLAY-OFF PRINCES

THE first time Argyle won promotion without finishing in the top three was also the first time they played at Wembley. On May 25th, 1996 – the latest date on which promotion has been achieved – Neil Warnock's side beat Darlington 1-0 in the 1995/96 Endsleigh Third Division play-off final thanks to Ronnie Maugé's second-half header. The Pilgrims' Wembley winners were: Steve Cherry, Mark Patterson, Paul Williams, Ronnie Maugé, Mick Heathcote, Martin Barlow, Chris Leadbitter, Richard Logan, Adrian Littlejohn, Michael Evans, Chris Curran.

MAUGÉ MAGIC

RONNIE Maugé cemented his place in Argyle folklore at around 4.10pm on May 25th 1996 at Wembley Stadium. It was at that moment that the midfielder rose to head home Mark Patterson's right-wing cross and secure a 1-0 win in the Third Division play-off final against Darlington. Ronnie arrived at Home Park in the summer of 1995 as Neil Warnock attempted to manage the Pilgrims back to the Endsleigh Second Division at the first time of asking. Ronnie scored 18 goals in 158 appearances for the Greens between 1995 and 1999, but none had the impact of the one at Wembley. After leaving Argyle, and joining up with future Pilgrims manager Ian Holloway at Bristol Rovers, he was called into the Trinidad and Tobago Gold Cup squad in 2000. Although the Soca Warriors reached the semi-finals, Ronnie broke his leg in a first-round match against Mexico, which led to his eventual retirement in 2002.

OUT WITH THE OLD

IN the 1985/86 promotion-winning season, New Year's Day was a case of out with the old. The 4-4 draw against Cardiff City at Home Park saw goalkeeper Geoff Crudgington badly injured; he gave way to understudy Dave Philp for the subsequent two matches on January 4th and January 7th. That was the first time since November 16th (seven league and two FA cup matches previously) that manager Dave Smith had to alter the starting XI of: Crudgington, Gordon Nisbet, Clive Goodyear, Gerry McElhinney, Leigh Cooper, Kevin Summerfield, Kevin Hodges, Russell Coughlin, Garry Nelson, Steve Cooper, John Clayton. That XI won five and drew two of the nine matches.

LEADER'S LANDMARK

ARGYLE'S 2,000th league strike came 16 seasons and 22 years later, in their opening home match of 1955/56, when they drew 2-2 against Doncaster Rovers. Player-manager Jack Rowley claimed the landmark strike with the Pilgrims' second goal of the game. The 3,000th league goal was claimed by left-winger Don Hutchins almost exactly 16 years after Rowley's 2,000th, on August 21st 1971, when he notched the winner in a 1-0 victory over Blackburn Rovers. Like Rowley's, it came in Argyle's opening home game of the Third Division campaign.

LEGENDS LASH OUT

THE Greens' 4,000th and 5,000th league goals were both claimed by living Argyle legends, with strikes that were a little out of the ordinary. Goal number 4,000 was scored by Team of the Century right-back Gordon Nisbet, 15 seasons after goal 3,000. It was the opening goal in a 5-0 Second Division thrashing of Grimsby Town at Home Park on March 21st 1987, a 25-yard screamer. Number 5,000 came in the Pilgrims' 2003-04 Nationwide Second Division title-winning season and is the only one of the landmark goals to be scored away from Home Park. It was claimed, 17 seasons after goal 4,000, by captain Paul Wotton at AFC Bournemouth on a blowy and wet Boxing Day. Wottsy nicked the ball from a breakdown in the centre-circle and lambasted it with power and precision to beat the opposition goalkeeper all ends up.

MARCHING ON...

THE earliest in the year that the Pilgrims have been promoted was in 2002, on Tuesday, 26th March, when Paul Sturrock's side made sure that they maintained a 21-week lead of the 2001/02 Nationwide Third Division with a come-from-behind 3-1 victory over Rochdale at Spotland. It was the first time a Pilgrims promotion-winning side had featured substitutes, with one of the three replacements, Marino Keith, scoring. Graham Coughlan and Lee Hodges ensured Second Division football with six matches of the season to spare. Argyle: Romain Larrieu, David Worrell, Steve Adams, Jason Bent, David Friio, Paul Wotton, Graham Coughlan, Michael Evans, Jon Beswetherick, Lee Hodges, Blair Sturrock. Substitutes: Ian Stonebridge, Marino Keith, Neil Heaney.

...AND ON

TWO years after Paul Sturrock's side moved from the Nationwide Third Division to the Second, a side fashioned by Sturrock was guided to the next level by Kevin Summerfield, who had remained at Home Park after Sturrock had joined Premiership Southampton with the finishing-post in sight. The win that clinched promotion to the first ever Championship in 2004-05 – and the title – came on April 24th 2004 at Home Park with a 2-0 win over promotion rivals Queens Park Rangers at Home Park with late goals at the Devonport end from Michael Evans and David Friio, two of five players that had featured in the Pilgrims' previous promotion-winning game, alongside Graham Coughlan, Lee Hodges and Marino Keith. Argyle: Luke McCormick, Paul Connolly, Graham Coughlan, Hasney Aljofree, Peter Gilbert, David Norris, David Friio, Lee Hodges, Tony Capaldi, Michael Evans, Marino Keith. Substitute: Nathan Lowndes.

SIMPLY SIMPSON

ARGYLE'S 1,000th Football League goal came in their 12th season, the 30th game of the 1932/33 Second Division campaign, when John Simpson scored the only goal of a home game against Stoke City. Simpson, who had scored once in his previous three games in his debut season, was badly injured in the subsequent game and had to retire as a result.

GRAHAM COUGHLAN: MEDALLION MAN

GETTING THE BIRD

PILGRIMS' winger Jimmy Hunter got the bird big time when the Pilgrims visited Carrow Road for a Second Division game against Norwich City on September 10th 1938. Hunter was about to score when, suddenly, a pigeon landed on the pitch and tripped up the Greens outside-right. He did recover sufficiently to get his shot in, but the moment had gone and the shot was saved. Argyle lost the game 2-1, Bill Hullett claiming a consolation goal.

SAME AGAIN, LADS

BETWEEEN January 6th and March 24th 1962, a run of ten Second Division games and two FA Cup ties, the Pilgrims sent out exactly the same XI. The Same Again Streak began at Home Park, where the line-up of Dave MacLaren, George Robertson, Bryce Fulton, Johnny Williams, Gordon Fincham, John Newman, Peter Anderson, Wilf Carter, George Kirby, Jimmy McAnearney and Ken Maloy put West Ham United out of the cup, 3-0, Carter, Williams and Maloy scoring. That same XI did duty in the Pilgrims' next 11 matches before manager Ellis Stuttard made a change. The settled line-up lost just two of the 12 matches, including a 5-1 FA Cup fourth-round thrashing by holders Tottenham Hotspur at Home Park, and won seven. Although they won the 13th game, when Dave Corbett replaced Maloy, the break to their rhythm saw a disastrous end to the season, with five defeats and a draw in their final six games. Despite this, the Pilgrims finished the campaign in fifth place – their second highest ever league placing. Incidentally, the Same Again XI were almost selected for a remarkable 18 games as they were also together for five of the six games prior to the run, with Robertson being replaced by the nearly-but-not-quite David Roberts for a 3-1 home thrashing of Norwich City on December 30th.

TEAMS ARGYLE HAVE MET MOST OFTEN

Bristol Rovers	125
Brentford	120
Millwall	113
Brighton	106
Southampton	104

THE FEW

THE FEWEST players Argyle have used in a season is 17, which was their entire squad for the 1951/52 Third Division (South) campaign. This motley crew included: reserve goalkeeper Les Major who was Bill Shortt's replacement in just two games; half-back Sid Rundle, who similarly played only two matches – he was coming to the end of his playing career then; inside-forward George Willis who likewise got stripped just twice, including on the opening day of the season; forward Harold Dobbie, who played in six matches; and winger Billy Strauss, who made nine appearances. That meant that manager Jimmy Rae used just 12 players to effectively shoulder responsibility for the entire campaign. It worked, too, as Argyle were promoted as champions. The trick was nearly repeated in 1968/69, when Billy Bingham used only 18 players in a Third Division season that saw the Pilgrims finish fifth. Striker John Wingate made only one Argyle appearance in that campaign – or, in fact, ever – Frank Lord played just six times, and John Tedesco eight times. The 17 were: Gordon Astall, Jack Chisholm, George Dews, Harold Dobbie, Neil Dougall, Alex Govan, Pat Jones, Tony McShane, Les Major, Johnny Porteous, Paddy Ratcliffe, Peter Rattray, Sid Rundle, Bill Shortt, Billy Strauss, Maurice Tadman, George Willis.

CAPALDI'S CAPS

TONY Capaldi holds the record for international caps won by a player while at Argyle (as opposed to international caps won by an Argyle player, otherwise Peter Shilton's 125 would be somewhere over the horizon). When the left-sided player won his 21st Northern Ireland cap against Wales in a 0-0 draw at Windsor Park on February 6th 2007, he overtook the mark set by Moses Russell, ironically a Welshman, at the beginning of the 20th century. Capaldi, who played 141 times for the Pilgrims, scoring 12 goals, had made his international debut in March 2004 in a 1-0 victory over Estonia. He memorably played in his country's famous 1-0 victory over England in September 2005, marking David Beckham. In a further Welsh international link to the Pilgrims, the first player from the club to be selected for international duty was a Welshman, Richard Morris, who played for his country in a 1-0 defeat to Ireland at Aberdare on April 11th 1908. Morris owed his call-up at least in part to the 12 goals he scored for the Pilgrims in the 1907/08 season which saw the Pilgrims end the campaign as runners-up.

KING KEV

NO-ONE has played more times for Plymouth Argyle – or is ever likely to – than Kevin Hodges, who can claim a place at the top table in the Pilgrims' banqueting hall on many counts. Not only did the midfielder and occasional full-back play 130 more times for the Greens than any other Pilgrim, he also gamely managed the club during one of the most turbulent times in its history. He was a member of the Third Division Argyle side that lost to Watford in the 1984 FA Cup semi-final at Villa Park (and, to this day, still cannot believe how his late shot somehow drifted wide) and was an ever-present as the Pilgrims won promotion to the Second Division two seasons later. He was leading scorer that season, with 16 goals, Player of the Year, and labelled 'a manager's dream' by often day-dreaming manager Dave Smith. In fact, between 1981 and 1986, he missed just six league matches. He was, naturally enough, a shoe-in for the Pilgrims' Team of the Century, voted for by fans in 2003-04. In December 1992, Hodgy signed for Torquay United, where he rose through the coaching ranks to become a successful first-team manager. He was poached back to Home Park in time for the 1998-99 season and, despite overwhelming odds, kept the team comfortably in mid-table of the Third Division for a couple of seasons before handing over the reins to Paul Sturrock. He remained close to the club, however, and in recent seasons, has helped out the youth team and Football in the Community department whenever his schedule has allowed.

Kevin Hodges 1978-1992	620
Sammy Black 1924-1938	491
Fred Craig 1912-1930	467
Johnny Williams 1955-1966	448
Jonny Hore 1964-1976	441
Pat Jones 1947-1958	441
Michael Evans 1991-1997 & 2001-2006	432
Paul Wotton 1994-2007	437
Jack Leslie 1921-1935	401
Moses Russell 1914-1929	400

BLACK MAGIC

SAMMY Black is another diminutive former Pilgrim whose record-breaking career with the Greens is never likely to be eclipsed. Certainly, if Argyle do discover another striker capable of scoring 184 goals in 491 league and cup matches, it will take something amazing for them to be able to keep hold of him. Black joined the Pilgrims from the splendidly named Kirkintilloch Rob Roy in 1924 and scored on his debut, a 7-1 drubbing of Swansea Town. Described by former Argyle director Michael Foot as 'the finest left-winger in an age of left-wingers' (and the former Labour Party leader should know a thing or two about left-wingers), Black was two-footed and precise in the shot. He was top scorer in five of the nine seasons between 1929 and 1936, including the 1929/30 Third Division (South) title-winning campaign, when his 21 goals earned him a benefit match – actually the last home game of the season, against Watford – which saw him presented with a cheque for £50 by the Mayor of Plymouth. Black's tally owed more to the longevity of his Home Park career, rather than sheer prolificness. During the Second World War, he worked as a storehouse assistant at the Royal Naval Armaments Depot in Plymouth, service that saw him awarded the Imperial Service Medal in 1966.

Player	Goals
Sammy Black 1924-1938	184
Wilf Carter 1957-1964	148
Tommy Tynan 1983-1985 & 1986-1990	145
Jack Leslie 1921-1935	136
Maurice Tadman 1947-1955	112
Jack Vidler 1928-1939	103
Raymond Bowden 1927-1933	87
Kevin Hodges 1978-1992	87
Mickey Evans 1991-1997 & 2001-2006	81
G Dews 1947-1955	81
Mike Bickle 1966-1971	74
Jack Cock 1925-1927	74
Bert Bowler 1912-1923	68
Paul Wotton 1994-2007	63
Paul Mariner 1973-1976	61

38 GUNS

THE 2000/2001 Nationwide Third Division season, at the start of which Paul Sturrock replaced Kevin Hodges as manager, saw 38 players share 669 appearances between them, the most ever to represent the Pilgrims in a single campaign. Several were Hodges players that Sturrock did not fancy when he took over (e.g. Adam Barrett, Kevin Nancekivell); others were try-outs that did not impress enough (e.g. Danny Bance, Jean-Philippe Javary); still others were loans (e.g. Robbie Betts, Lee Wilkie); and there was a fair smattering of youngsters given their head prior to greater things (e.g. Paul Connolly, Luke McCormick). Sturrock's tinkering paid dividends the following season when, having satisfied himself of the good and the bad among the 38, he put together a squad that won the division. The 38 were: Steve Adams, Danny Bance, Martin Barlow, Adam Barrett, Jon Beswetherick, Robert Betts, Paul Connolly, Stuart Elliott, Michael Evans, Sean Evers, Terry Fleming, David Friio, Steve Guinan, Martin Gritton, Mick Heathcote, John Hodges, Jean-Philippe Javary, Romain Larrieu, Chris Leadbitter, Paul Mardon, Sean McCarthy, Luke McCormack, Brian McGlinchey, Paul McGregor, Michael Meaker, Kevin Nancekivell, Wayne O'Sullivan, Jason Peak, Lee Phillips, Martin Phillips, Jon Sheffield, Ian Stonebridge, Craig Taylor, Ryan Trudgian, Lee Wilkie, Kevin Wills, David Worrell, and Paul Wotton.

SEMI DETACHED

IT is largely forgotten, in light of Argyle's 1-0 FA Cup semi-final defeat in 1983/84, that they reached the last four of another knockout competition that season, the Associate Members' Cup. While the Pilgrims were progressing to the verge of becoming the first Third Division side to reach an FA Cup Final, they were also concurrently working their way through a bunch of lower division sides in the first year of the unsponsored tournament. All four of their games were played at Home Park. After thrashing Torquay United 5-1, they beat Brentford 2-0 to earn a quarter-final place against Exeter City. They saw the Grecians off 2-1 to book a last-four place against Millwall on May 17th but, just like their other semi-final, they lost 1-0 in front of a crowd less than a tenth of the size than the one at Villa Park. The following two seasons saw the Pilgrims establish themselves as not very good Associate Members' Cup fighters. Before they were promoted to the Second Division, they played twice in the (by now) Freight Rover Trophy, dipping out after the group stage.

STARTING ORDERS AND END GAMES

IN their second season in the Football League, the Pilgrims suffered only one defeat in their first 17 Third Division (South) matches and one defeat in their last 17 games of the season. That was on the closing day, at Queens Park Rangers, and it cost Argyle the title as they missed promotion on goal difference. In the 1925/26 Third Division (South) season, the Pilgrims won both their opening two games 6-2, both at home, against Southend United and Crystal Palace. That campaign also included two 7-2 wins and a 5-5 draw, but the Pilgrims ended up only runners-up. Argyle finished the 1934/35 Second Division season in eighth place, a remarkable achievement considering they managed only one win in their first ten matches; in 1937/38, they won their first match but did not taste victory in the subsequent 11 games on their way to finishing 13th in the Second Division. In 1946/47, the Pilgrims lost 11 of their last 12 matches to end up 19th in the Second Division, while relegation to the Third Division (South) in 1949/50 was not a surprise after they opened up with a draw and seven defeats from their first eight games. In 1952/53, the Pilgrims did not lose until their eighth match, eventually ending up fourth in the Second Division, their highest finishing league position; in 1953/54, they did not win until their eighth game and finished only six places worse off. In 1961/62, the Greens lost five and drew one of the last six matches to finished fifth in the Second Division, only five points behind the second promoted team, Leyton Orient; in 1963/64, Argyle did not win until the 12th match and had no wins in the last five matches, but finished safe in 20th position. In 1981/82, the Pilgrims lost 10 and drew 2 of their first 12 matches, but finished 16th in the Third Division while, in 1985/86, they won 13 and drew two of their last 16 games to storm to promotion to the Second Division carrying that form on to the higher level, not suffering defeat the following season until their 10th game – for an aggregate of one defeat in 25 games. In the 1997/98 Nationwide Second Division season, the Pilgrims managed only one win up until November 1st and were eventually relegated; while in 2001/02, they did not win any of their first three Nationwide Third Division games but went on to win the league… with 102 points from the next 129 available.

LACK OF GLASS

FOR their entire participation in the Autoglass Trophy/Auto Windscreens Shield/LDV Vans Trophy, the Pilgrims failed to make much of an impression. From 1992/93, when they finished third in a group after drawing with Exeter City (1-1) and losing to Torquay United (2-1), to 1999, when they were beaten 1-0 by Torquay, Argyle lost seven of their ten games in the competition. They won only twice in that time, both times in 1996/97, when they reached the quarter-final of what used to be known as the Associate Members' Cup but cannot be any longer because the tournament is, in fact, an anachronism as there is now no distinction between full and associate membership of the Football League. Having beaten AFC Bournemouth (2-0) and Brighton & Hove Albion (1-0) in front of a combined Home Park gate of less than 2,250, they went down 2-0 to Northampton Town, who had also beaten them the previous year, and did so again the following season, 5-3 on penalties following a 1-1 draw. Even when Paul Sturrock's side was rampaging up the divisions, their form in the tournament only marginally improved: although there were some memorable wins – well, two, actually – both against Bristol City at Home Park, 3-0 in 2000 and 2003. There were also spectacular defeats, notably 3-0 at Bristol Rovers in 2000, and a home penalty shoot-out loss to Wycombe Wanderers in 2003. The Pilgrims eventually solved their poor form in the tournament by extricating themselves from the two lowest leagues and thus becoming ineligible to participate.

TABLES TURNED

DURING the 2001/02 season, Nationwide Third Division Argyle's chief executive David Tall was subject of a TV series called *Turning the Tables*. David swapped places with Steve Sutherland, the commercial director of then Premier League Charlton Athletic for a programme comparing two similar sized clubs at different levels in the league structure. David spent time at the Valley, learning how the big boys went about their big business, while Steve came to Home Park to pass on his expertise to Argyle's comparatively tiny – but ambitious – staff. Unlikely as it seemed then, the tables did, indeed, turn before the end of the decade. By the final day of the 2008/09 season, Argyle had come up from the fourth tier to the second; Charlton had dropped from the first to the third.

FULL OF NOTHING

BEFORE their fairly abject showing in the Associate Members' Cup, Argyle had failed to rip up any trees in its sister competition, the Full Members' Cup. They did not win a game in the first four years of the competition, starting off with a 3-2 loss at Ipswich Town in 1986/87. This was a relative success compared to the following two years when, with the competition now sponsored by Italian sportswear company Simod, they twice lost 6-2, at Manchester City, in 1987/88, and Chelsea, in 1988/89. A change of sponsors so that the tournament became the snappily titled Zenith Data Systems Cup, marginally improved the Pilgrims' fortunes in 1989/90; they lost only 5-2 to West Ham United, and this after being level at 90 minutes. The following year, they held Brighton & Hove Albion 0-0 at Home Park before going out in the penalty shoot-out. The improvement continued in 1991/92, when they reached the area quarter-final after Home Park victories over Portsmouth (1-0) and Millwall (4-0). It was third time unlucky when a Southampton side containing Alan Shearer and Matt Le Tissier tipped them out of the competition 1-0.

RIGHT CHARLIE

OLYMPIAN Charlie Twissell is the only Pilgrim to have represented Great Britain at football, in the Melbourne games of 1956. Charlie was an amateur for the Royal Navy who was signed for Argyle by manager Jack Rowley on amateur forms and played whenever he could get leave. The quick right-winger then bought himself out of the navy but retained his amateur status. He was selected for England's non-professional team and won six caps, against Ireland and Iceland in 1956, and Wales, Scotland, France and Bulgaria, in 1957. Charlie was an 'even-timer' on the running track, an accomplished long jumper, and one of the 200 athletes (176 men and 24 women) that Great Britain took to Melbourne in November 1956. The football team's first-round match was against Thailand, which they won 9-0, with Charlie scoring the first two goals. In the quarter-final, Team GB lost 6-1 to one of the favourites, Bulgaria, thus going out of the tournament. Bulgaria themselves went out in the semi-final to the eventual gold-medallists Russia, who included goalkeeper Lev Yashin in their line-up. Charlie did eventually turn professional, and, after two seasons with Argyle (42 appearances, nine goals) moved to York City.

BARNSLEY BAR

IN the 2008/09 Championship season, Argyle forward Rory Fallon was involved in every league and cup match except for two – the home and away league matches against Barnsley, where he started his career.

THE BEST OF TEAMS...

IT is an enduring debate among football fans of any club – which team is the best to have worn the colours over the years? And which is the worst? Well, the following stats might settle a few issues, although I think they could just add fuel to the fire, rather than quell it. In our quest for the best, you would have a pretty strong argument for nominating Paul Sturrock's Nationwide Third Division champions of 2001/02. For starters, they accrued more points in that campaign than any other Pilgrims side, a club and divisional record of 102. Even allowing for adjustment to take into account the different distribution of points, they still pip Bob Jack's 1929/30 Third Division (South) title-winners on what Luggy would call 'pointage'. In addition, they conceded fewer goals in their season than any other Greens team apart from the 1921/22 Third Division (South) runners-up, who played four fewer matches. The Sturrock side would have to give best on goal average, but would claim superiority on goal difference. Tantalisingly, the two generations are cigarette-paper close on numbers of wins and defeats during the campaign (remembering that the 21st century boys would have played four more matches). The 1929/30 team suffered fewer defeats – four to the 2001/02 side's six – but the modern generation can brag about one more win – 31 to 30. In terms of goals scored, the 1929/30 side sits fourth on the all-time list, with 98, which is the length of Royal Parade better than the 2001/02's 71 (and, to add spice to any argument about the different eras, let it be recalled that Luton Town finished runners-up in 2001-02 with 96 goals). Both have to give best to three other seasons, two of which involved at least a few of the 1929/30 side: 1925/26 and 1951/52, in each of which the Argyle strikers scored 107 goals; and 1931/32, when a tally of exactly 100 was reached. Mention of Jimmy Rae's 1951/52 Third Division (South) title-winners throws up another contender for the all-time Pilgrims best side: prolific scorers, major points gatherers, hard to beat – they tick almost all the boxes. Jack, Rae and Sturrock – what is it about the Scots and management, eh?

...THE WORST OF TEAMS

AS for the worst ever Pilgrims side, it would be impossible to argue against the 1945/46 side that played in post Second World War Football League (South). For a city brought to its knees by a continual night after night blitzkrieg bombardment, simply competing was a triumph, and the fact that the club used 72 players during the campaign did not do much for a settled team. Apart from that season, Argyle have four times suffered 24 defeats in a seasons – 1991/1992, 1994/1995, 1955/1956 and 1967/1968 – campaigns which the more astute among you will have noticed, ended in relegation. The 1967/68 side that finished bottom of the Second Division under the management of, first, Derek Ufton and, then, Billy Bingham, actually scored fewer goals than the 1945/46 side – 38 to 39 – but not as few as the 35 scored by the Pilgrims in their first season in the Football League, the 1920/21 Third Division side. Maybe, though, lack of goals does not necessarily make for an unsuccessful season: the 39 total was matched by the side that eventually finished comfortably mid-table in the 2005/06 Coca-Cola Championship. Unsurprisingly, the 1967/68 team places in the top (bottom?) ten on fewest points (27) and fewest wins (nine). Difficult to perceive that as anything else but poor, really. Other years which were apparently not particularly halcyon for Greens were 1955/56, when Jack Rowley's side exited the Second Division at the wrong end, and the preceding 1954/55 campaign when, obviously, they did not. Almost, though.

BOOM TIME

THE total number of spectators that watched Argyle at Home Park during the 1951/52 season was 442,417; 105,309 witnessed the reserve matches.

WELL PRACTICED

RECEIPTS from Argyle's practice matches in 1920 totalled £197 17s 0d, which was donated to local hospitals.

ARMS AND THE MAN

ARGYLE forward Tommy Gallogley's party trick was to stand with his arms out wide and let his nephews swing on them.

GREASE IS THE WORD

THERE were various 'anomalies' that used to be taken for granted in Argyle's early days which would not be tolerated – to say the least – in today's game. For instance, when the Pilgrims were planning on becoming professional and joining the Southern League in 1903, manager Frank Brettell reported to the directors that he had interviewed most of the league secretaries and discovered that the majority would require a financial inducement to vote in favour of the Pilgrims' application. Argyle were voted into the Southern League but extra payments did not end there – one of the conditions of entry was that, during the first season, the travelling expenses incurred by visiting teams had to be paid by Argyle.

ICE WORK

DURING Argyle's brief spell under manager Tony Pulis in 2005/06, he intensified the training routine. Part of his routine was to have the players jump into a wheelie-bin full of ice.

NO-ONE HOME

IT was not only Tony Pulis who had strange ideas. His successor, Ian Holloway, wanted Smeaton's Tower, the lighthouse on the famous Plymouth Hoe, to be painted in the team's green and white colours. The Tower's red and white was too reminiscent of Exeter City and Bristol City.

CHAT'S THE WAY

DAVE Smith takes the biscuit when it comes to eccentricity. The 1980s manager used to borrow the pitchside announcer's microphone to talk to the crowd before a home match. If he did not have any important message to announce, he would often recite poetry.

FRIIO'S A JOLLY GOOD FELLOW

ARGYLE'S French midfielder David Friio won the Umbro Isotonic Second Division Player of the Month award for November 2003 – the only Pilgrim ever to be so honoured.

HIGHER HOME PARK

ARGYLE chairman Dan McCauley also raised a few eyebrows at Home Park. No eyebrows were raised higher than those of local journalists who, having been refused entry to Home Park in the mid 1990s after upsetting Dan, resorted to hiring a cherry-picker and parked it outside the ground to raise them 200 feet in the air to see over the ground.

THE BEAUTIFUL GAME

BACK in the day, there used to be a Miss Plymouth Argyle – a very non-PC beauty contest, not a Saturday afternoon habit. The most well-known couple were Mary Firmin, from 1970, and Toni-Marie Germaine, in 1985.

AVON CALLING

IN June 1924 Argyle sailed on RMS *Avon* to tour South America, where they won three of their nine matches, lost three matches and (for those of you who really cannot be bothered with mental arithmetic) drew three matches. One of the more interesting matches of this tour was against Boca Juniors in Buenos Aires. Boca scored first, which invited a pitch invasion and the supporters carried all eleven players shoulder high. The Argyle players had to leave the pitch until order could be restored, and when the match continued the referee – who just happened to be a Plymothian, Fred Reeve – awarded Argyle a penalty. This was a cue for another pitch invasion and the players had to go off again. While in the safety of the dressing-room, the players decided that enough was enough and developed a strategy whereby Patsy Corcoran would take the penalty, and deliberately miss it. When they returned to the cauldron, team-mate Moses Russell had different plans, pushed Corcoran aside, and scored. Guess what? Another pitch invasion – and the match was abandoned.

HEAD DON

GEORGE Taylor, Argyle's assistant manager in the 1950s, scored the winning goal for Aberdeen when they beat Rangers in the Scottish League Cup Final at Hampden in 1946.

GOALKEEPER TURNED POACHER

JACK Robinson, Argyle's goalkeeper in 1904/05, was not re-engaged for the following season. He was, however, the referee for Argyle's first game of 1905/06.

POACHED TURNED STRONGMAN

ARCHIE Goodall joined Argyle from Derby in 1903, but had to return to Derby when the FA considered he was poached. After retiring as a player, Goodall travelled Europe and the United States as part of a strongman act before settling in London, where he lived out his remaining years.

RIPPER

IN 1925, Argyle's Bert Batten went on tour with the FA to Australia. On that tour, he scored a record 37 goals, surpassing the feat of William Hibbert, formerly of Newcastle United, who scored 32 goals in South Africa in 1910. Six of the goals came in a single match.

TERRACE TERRORS

THE biggest English crowd Argyle have ever played in front of – the 65,386 that witnessed their 4-2 1932 FA Cup fourth round defeat by Arsenal at Highbury – had suffered a number of problems. *The Western Independent* reported: "Half-an-hour before the start, the gates had to be closed, and the Arsenal management telephoned to the underground railways asking them to stop any more bookings, except for those people who had reserved seats. Before the game, there were some amazing happenings on the high terraces behind each of the goals. Packed masses of humanity swayed dangerously time after time, and it really looked as though someone might be seriously hurt. There were fainting cases galore, and the crowd was so dense that it was impossible for the ambulance men to get to them. Consequently, people on the higher part of the terraces who fainted had to be lifted over the heads of the crowd, and bundled – there is no other word for it – unceremoniously down to the playing area, still over heads of the crowd all the time. At least one man had his leg broken in this way, and it looked as though others must have been injured as well."

PENALTY KICKS

IT is unlikely that very many people who saw Argyle's League Cup tie against Aston Villa at Home Park on February 6th 1961 could tell you the score... but almost everyone in the ground will be able to recall the Pilgrims' second goal. It was scored by Johnny Newman, after Wilf Carter had already put Argyle one goal up, when the Pilgrims were awarded a dubious 36th-minute penalty when the Villa half-back Vic Crowe tried to play as goalkeeper and punch the ball clear. Villa's proper goalkeeper Nigel Sims saved Carter's spot-kick but the referee ordered it to be re-taken due to an infringement. Carter then became worried that Sims could psyche him out so he had a word with Johnny Newman about a penalty routine they had tried on the training ground. Second time around, Carter merely tapped the ball forward and Newman ran on to it and struck it home. The Villa manager at this time was the former Arsenal and Everton left-half Joe Mercer, who liked the routine so much that he and Newman later performed the trick when they played together in an All-Stars XI. Oh, and Villa won the game 5-3. Told you that you didn't remember.

BACK IN THE OLD ROUTINE

ARGYLE reprised the Carter-Newman penalty routine in a Second Division game against Manchester City at Home Park on November 21st 1964. Again, it came from a controversial penalty decision for the Pilgrims, and again Newman was involved. This time, though, his partner in crime was Mike Trebilcock. This time, there was no re-take. Argyle captain Newman simply placed the ball and got ready for what looked like a normal spot-kick. However, he merely tapped it forward a few feet and Trebilcock – who must have rehearsed the move with Newman – ran onto the ball and hit it past Alan Ogley in the Manchester City goal. The City players protested, but Luton referee David Wells said that this was perfectly legal because (a) the ball was played forward and (b) Trebilcock, running in, could not have been offside as he was behind the ball when it was played. All very entertaining, but was it original? Not if you accept the word of the *Western Morning News* reporter 'Tamar', who said: "Argyle put the clock back to the footballing days of Raich Carter and Peter Doherty, who used this method."

THROWING THE GAME

THE oddest goal scored at Home Park? Try this one for size. On October 2nd 1954, Argyle went into their Second Division game with Fulham, having only won once since the beginning of the season. During the game, Fulham goalkeeper Frank Elliott was challenged for the ball by Argyle's Neil Langman, a man into whose eyes no-one would kick sand. The challenge left Elliott in agony on the ground and, being in so much pain and confused, he just flung the ball out of play. Or so he thought. The ball merely went into his own goal. To add injury to injury, he had a broken wrist, so former Manchester United outside-left Charlie Mitten took over in goal and did an excellent job, but constant Argyle pressure told in the end and, thanks to further goals from Johnny Porteous and Tony McShane, they ran out 3-2 winners against the ten men from Fulham. Incidentally, Charlie's son, John, played 46 times for the Pilgrims between 1967 and 1968, scoring eight goals.

PLAY TO THE WHISTLE

ARGYLE beat Everton 1-0 in a Second Division game at Home Park on November 15th 1952 without scoring. Leastways, that is what the opposition players thought. Argyle midfielder Neil Dougall's late long-range shot is what separated the two teams, but it came after Dougall had apparently been fouled and recovered his footing. The Everton players stopped playing, convinced they had heard a whistle blown for a free-kick, and swarmed around the referee, protesting. However, the goal stood, with Neil shrugging that he never heard anything – apart from the roar that greeted his winning strike.

HARD MAN

GIL Merrick, the Birmingham and England goalkeeper, once said that, in his opinion, the hardest shot in football belonged to Neil Dougall, who played 290 times for the Pilgrims, scoring 26 goals, between 1949 and 1960 before moving upstairs to become manager.

COMING HOME

OF the players on Argyle's books prior to the First World War, no fewer than 15 resumed after the conflict.

PLYMOUTH WEDNESDAY

ARGYLE'S 'A' team finished as champions of the Devon Wednesday Senior League in 1950. Their only defeat was to RAF Collaton Cross at Yealmpton.

BUSY BEES

IN Argyle's ignominious Football League (South) season of 1945/46, they conceded a goal to Brentford within 15 seconds of their game at Home Park on April 6th. The match ended 1-1, with Bill Hurst scoring for the Pilgrims.

HAVE GLOVES...

GOALKEEPER Rab Douglas played for Plymouth Argyle despite never visiting Plymouth. The 19-times capped Scottish international was signed for the Pilgrims by Paul Sturrock on an emergency loan from Leicester City to play in a Championship game against Bristol City at Ashton Gate on March 15th 2008. The emergency had been caused by Luke McCormick's sending off at Scunthorpe United four days earlier which left Sturrock with one suspended goalkeeper and another – Romain Larrieu – injured. Showing he bore his old club no malice, Leicester manager Ian Holloway arranged for Rab to meet up with his temporary colleagues at a Bristol hotel on the eve of the game, which the Pilgrims won 2-1 thanks to two Rory Fallon strikes. After the match, and with McCormick now available again, Rab travelled straight back to Leicester.

FERRY NICE

ARGYLE midfielder Aiden Maher was riding Plymouth's Torpoint Ferry when a runaway pram containing a baby charged down the slipway into the water. Aiden – who played 70 times for the Pilgrims, scoring three goals, between 1968 and 1971 – and a policeman jumped into the water, risking serious injury to save the baby, one Leanne Goddard. It is usually a goalkeeper who makes saves, but Leanne was saved by a left-winger.

SPOT ON

FRED Craig, Argyle's goalkeeper in the 1920s, used to take the occasional penalty for Argyle, scoring five in total in a staggering 466 first-team appearances between 1912 and 1930. His technique was simple, and not unlike that of Paul Wotton some 80 years later. Smash it. Against Newport County, in a 4-1 Third Division (South) victory at Home Park on January 15th 1927, his ferocious shot broke the net.

JOINT PROJECT

WHEN he was not allowing small relatives to swing from his arms, forward Tommy Gallogley's party trick was to use the railings at Home Park to put his knee out of its socket. This was a rather painful sounding ruse that Tommy – who played 136 times for the Pilgrims between 1913 and 1923, scoring 26 goals – used to his advantage when called for a medical for the First World War.

DADS' BARMY

ARGYLE'S 1984 FA Cup semi-final against Watford at Aston Villa was noted for its good behaviour from both sets of supporters, but there were two men who were escorted away from Villa Park in a police car – the father of Argyle midfielder Kevin Hodges and his dad's friend. The two elderly gentlemen had come out of the ground and walked in the general direction that most of the others were walking, only to realise that they could not find their coaches and were with the Watford fans. They stopped and asked directions from a policeman, who could not understand how they had ended up where they had ended up – he called for a police car which took them to their coach.

POTTY PLAYER

FRANK Arundel, whose nickname was 'Chick' and who played four matches at outside-left for Argyle between 1956 and 1959, was a skilful and tricky player on the Greens' pitch and on the green baize. Frank was regarded as more than a quite useful snooker player.

TEAM OF TEAMS

HOW about this for a Pilgrims team of teams? Geoff BARNSLEY (1957-61; 131 appearances), George SHEFFIELD (1920-21; 19 appearances, 4 goals), Jon SHEFFIELD (1997-2001; 155 appearances), Bob PRESTON (1923-1928; 140 appearances, 3 goals), Jim HAMILTON (1976; 8 appearances), George FORREST (1933-34; 3 appearances), Pat GLOVER (1939-40; 9 appearances, 6 goals), Barry SILKMAN (1978-79; 15 appearances, 2 goals), Alan MILLER (1988-89; 15 appearances), Paul MARINER (1973-76; 155 appearances, 60 goals), Steve CHERRY (1986-89; 102 appearances).

GOALS-BOYS

BALL-BOYS were first used at Home Park in 1932, although they were called 'goal-boys' then.

GREEN PARTY

DIRECTOR Michael Foot is not the only Argyle fan from the world of politics. One-time Foreign Secretary Dr. David Owen took a big interest in the Pilgrims, as did Plymouth Drake MP between 1974-97 Janet Fookes; Alan Clark, the MP for Plymouth Sutton between 1974-89; and Robert Hicks, the Bodmin MP between 1970-83 and for South East Cornwall between 1983-97.

DOWN ON LUCK

IN terms of league position, the worst decade in the Pilgrims' history was the 1990s. Peter Shilton's Argyle were relegated from the Barclays Second Division in 1992… to the Barclays Second Division. The league system was rearranged because of the introduction of the Premiership. Three seasons later, the Pilgrims were relegated to the fourth tier of the English game (now the Third Division) for the first time in their history, bounced back immediately under Neil Warnock in 1995/96, but went back down again under Warnock's old assistant Mick Jones after two further seasons. They remained down among the dead men until the third season of the new millennium.

GOOD TIMES

ARGYLE used to run a match-day raffle where the match-ball was the prize. Fans would arrive at Home Park to be greeted by people selling tickets with the exhortation: "Tuppence on the match ball – four for sixpence." Supporters buying a ticket (or four for sixpence) would find a time printed on it in minutes and seconds. If the time on the ticket matched the time of the first goal, the ticket-holder won the ball. However, getting the seconds correct was nigh-on impossible, and – here is a shock – it was usually the club that was the winner with an unclaimed prize.

SAVE OUR SAMMY

AT one time, when finances were tight (when were they not?) Argyle were in danger of losing left-winger Sammy Black, a player who would have graced any top-flight team of the day and described by Argyle director and lifelong fan Michael Foot as "the finest player I ever saw in Argyle's green shirt" – and he has seen a few. A fundraising evening was held at the Guildhall, in Plymouth city centre, dubbed an 'SOS Meeting' – Save Our Sammy. Arsenal manager George Allison visited Plymouth to address the supporters at the meeting, where Argyle shares were also on sale…and Sammy was duly saved.

BAND OF GREEN

FOR many years in the 1950s, the territorial band used to play before matches at Home Park, bandmaster A. W. Lowther leading the troop.

PILGRIM BROTHERS

WHEN brothers Neil and Peter Langman joined Argyle from Tavistock in the 1950s, the Pilgrims struck an unusual deal with the Devon non-league side. The Pilgrims gave Tavistock £350 on the understanding that they would be given the first opportunity to sign any future Tavi player and use the facilities at the Lambs' Langsford Park ground when they were playing away from home. It was money well invested: defender Peter played 93 times for the Pilgrims between 1951 and 1957, while forward Neil netted 50 goals in 100 matches between 1953 and 1957.

ON THE MARCH

THE Argyle theme tune is Semper Fidelis, a march written in 1888 by John Philip Sousa, a U. S. composer known particularly for American patriotic marches, of which he wrote 136, including Stars and Stripes Forever, the national march of the United States; the Washington Post; and the Liberty Bell, otherwise known as the theme for *Monty Python's Flying Circus* (but not including the raspberry). Semper Fidelis is Latin for 'Always Faithful' and is the motto of the United States Marine Corps – often shortened to Semper Fi – adopted in 1883, on the initiative of Colonel Charles McCawley. Before that, it was a motto used widely by families in Great Britain and Ireland, notably those of Scottish and Irish descent. The City of Exeter – Argyle's most deadly rivals – has used the motto since at least 1660 on the instigation of Queen Elizabeth I in recognition of a gift of money toward the fleet that had defeated the Spanish Armada. The motto is also used by the Royal Navy HMS *Exeter*, which was named after the City of Exeter; by various Exeter-based units of the British Army; and there is a Masonic Lodge in Exeter called 'Lodge Semper Fidelis'. Other diverse places that use Semper Fidelis as their motto are: the Ukrainian city of Lviv; the town of St. Malo, in Brittany, France; and the city of White Plains, in New York, United States. The 1st (Exeter and South Devon) Rifle Volunteer Corps, raised in Exeter in 1852, was using the motto on its cap badge by 1860 and it was adopted by the Devonshire Regiment of the British Army on its formation from the South and North Devon militias in 1881. The motto was further continued on the badges of the Devonshire and Dorset Regiment when the Devonshires were amalgamated into them in 1958. These regiments had a base in Exeter until their disappearance by amalgamation in 2007. Semper Fidelis is also the motto of: the West Nova Scotia Regiment of the Canadian Forces; the cadets corps from the Dutch Royal Military Academy; the 11th Infantry Regiment of the United States Army; Canadian Forces Base Valcartier; a Swiss Grenadier regiment formed in 1943; the Republic of China Marine Corps; the Hungarian Government Guard; the 1st company of the Brazilian Military Institute of Engineering; the Romanian Protection and Guard Service, a company which is concerned with the national security and personal security of officials in Romania; the Submarine Force of the Chilean Navy; but not Argyle, which does not seem to have a club motto.

GLOVE STORY

THE first substitute goalkeeper used by the Pilgrims was Ray Newland. The Liverpudlian custodian replaced Alan Nicholls in a Barclays Second Division game at Barnet on February 12th 1994. To be more accurate, he replaced midfielder Wayne Burnett, after Nicholls was sent off. Neither goalkeeper – both Peter Shilton protégés – conceded a goal, and none of Argyle's players scored, either, as the match ended 0-0. Newland went on to make another 28 appearances (all starts) for the Pilgrims before leaving for Chester City in 1994. After retiring, following a peripatetic career that also took in Torquay United, he set up a successful goalkeeper coaching company 'Just 4 Keepers'. In 2006, he launched its first international franchise in Canada.

IRON WILL

ARGYLE'S tour of Poland and East Germany in the early summer of 1963 was an eventful one. When the Pilgrims played KSC Lech in Poznan on May 18th, the match ball was dropped in by a helicopter. A nice idea, but the ball was too soft so the referee had to call for another one. At Gdansk three days later, after a 3-0 win over BWKS Lechia in which Wilf Carter, Jimmy McAnearney and Alan O'Neill scored, Argyle goalkeeper Dave MacLaren, who was also a pianist, led the Pilgrims players and guests at their hotel in a selection of English and Scottish songs after breakfast one morning. The coach which took the Argyle party to the airport for their flight home from the tour broke down. The East German interpreter said: "Perhaps the Russians want to keep you here." The Argyle players were initially not sure whether it was a joke, and were relieved when they were eventually flown out.

HOPPING MAD

CORNISH-BORN forward Ray Bowden, who played more than 150 games for the Pilgrims before becoming Arsenal's club record £5,000 signing in 1933, was a perfectly balanced two-footed player, an attribute he put down to his formative years when he hopped on one leg all the way to school, then hopped all the way home on the other. Bowden, who ran a successful sports shop in Plymouth after he retired, was apparently distressed at being called into the Argyle first team after joining them from Looe as it meant "putting a married man out of a job".